MINIMUM STANDARDS

FOR WILDLIFE REHABILITATION

Fourth Edition, 2012

Edited by Erica A. Miller, DVM

Preferred citation:

**Miller, E.A., editor. 2012. *Minimum Standards for Wildlife Rehabilitation, 4th edition.*
National Wildlife Rehabilitators Association, St. Cloud, MN. 116 pages.**

First Edition published 1989
Second Edition published 1993
Third Edition published 2000
Fourth Edition published 2012

ISBN 978-1-931439-28-2

International Wildlife Rehabilitation Council
PO Box 3197
Eugene, OR 97403 USA
(866) 871-1869
office@theiwrc.org
www.theiwrc.org

National Wildlife Rehabilitators Association
2625 Clearwater Road, Suite 110
St. Cloud, MN 56301 USA
(320) 230-9920
NWRA@nwrawildlife.org
www.nwrawildlife.org

ACKNOWLEDGEMENTS

The wildlife rehabilitators listed below have designed the various sections of this document. Their task was to compose a document and then reach a consensus with colleagues. This was no small task, and we thank them for their many efforts. Members of both organizations were encouraged to contribute; many individual rehabilitators sent in their suggestions, comments and concerns, all of which helped to make this a better document. Those who made significant contributions include: Mathias Engelman, Harriet Forrester, Susan Heckley, Harry Kelton, Nonda Surrat, and Regina Whitman.Special thanks to Tracy Leaver, the chair of the NWRA Standards Committee for several years, as she initiated this process, and then gathered and sorted the many letters that were submitted. Thanks, also, to Di Conger, Lessie Davis, Cheryl Hoggard, DVM, Diane Nickerson, Louise Shimmel, Elaine Thrune, and Sandy Woltman, whose editing helped make the document clear and understandable. Typesetting and layout was done by Erica Miller, DVM.

The concept of standards for wildlife rehabilitation and much of the original work was accomplished in the early 1980s by: Pat Adams, Curt Clumpner, Betsy Crozer, Mary Forness, Lynne Frink, MA, Pixie and Robert Goodrich, Michelle Green, IWRC Board of Directors 1982 and 1983, Susan Kelly, John Mulder, DVM, Carol Odel, Vaughan Pratt, DVM, Basil Tangredi, DVM, Kris Thorne-Bolduc, Jan White, DVM, and Linda Wolf, DVM.

The third edition (2000) of *Minimum Standards for Wildlife Rehabilitation* resulted from the suggestions and contributions of many wildlife rehabilitators via letters, phone calls, email messages, and conversations at national and regional conferences. Significant contributions were made by the following individuals: Wendy Aeschliman, Lori Arent, Ann Bradshaw, Susan Barnard, Allan & Shirley Casey, Curt Clumpner, Michael Cox, Lessie Davis, Marge Gibson, Robyn Graboski, Deirdre Goodfriend, Frank Gould, Sandy Heyn, Patrice Klein, VMD, Amanda Lollar, Daniel Ludwig, PhD, Bea Orendorff, Clyde Peeling, Mike Pratt, Louise Shimmel, Barbara Suto, Florina Tseng, DVM, and Regina Whitman.

DEDICATION

This edition of *Minimum Standards for Wildlife Rehabilitation* is dedicated to the memory of Wendy Fox. From her presentation "Mimimum Standards for Wildlife Rehabilitation--It's All About You" (2004) to every aspect of her work relating to wildlife rehabilitation, Wendy was a proponent of using these guidelines to "raise our efficiency and improve the level of care we provide [to wildlife]."

TABLE OF CONTENTS

LIST OF TABLES

CODE OF ETHICS

A Wildlife Rehabilitator's Code of Ethics

1. A wildlife rehabilitator should strive to achieve high standards of animal care through knowledge and an understanding of the field. Continuing efforts must be made to keep informed of current rehabilitation information, methods, and regulations.

2. A wildlife rehabilitator should be responsible, conscientious, and dedicated, and should continuously work toward improving the quality of care given to wild animals undergoing rehabilitation.

3. A wildlife rehabilitator must abide by local, state, provincial and federal laws concerning wildlife, wildlife rehabilitation, and associated activities.

4. A wildlife rehabilitator should establish safe work habits and conditions, abiding by current health and safety practices at all times.

5. A wildlife rehabilitator should acknowledge limitations and enlist the assistance of a veterinarian or other trained professional when appropriate.

6. A wildlife rehabilitator should respect other rehabilitators and persons in related fields, sharing skills and knowledge in the spirit of cooperation for the welfare of the animals.

7. A wildlife rehabilitator should place optimum animal care above personal gain.

8. A wildlife rehabilitator should strive to provide professional and humane care in all phases of wildlife rehabilitation, respecting the wildness and maintaining the dignity of each animal in life and in death. Releasable animals should be maintained in a wild condition and released as soon as appropriate. Non-releasable animals which are inappropriate for education, foster-parenting, or captive breeding have a right to euthanasia.

9. A wildlife rehabilitator should encourage community support and involvement through volunteer training and public education. The common goal should be to promote a responsible concern for living beings and the welfare of the environment.

10. A wildlife rehabilitator should work on the basis of sound ecological principles, incorporating appropriate conservation ethics and an attitude of stewardship.

11. A wildlife rehabilitator should conduct all business and activities in a professional manner, with honesty, integrity, compassion, and commitment, realizing that an individual's conduct reflects on the entire field of wildlife rehabilitation.

Message from the Presidents

Throughout 1999, I had the honor of working with a team of dedicated wildlife rehabilitators to compile and edit the 3rd edition of *Minimum Standards for Wildlife Rehabilitation*. Members of the joint Standards Committee of NWRA and IWRC again worked together in 2004-2011 to compile information for this updated 4th edition. Rather than a new letter of introduction, I would encourage you to read the letter below, which was written by the NWRA and IWRC Presidents at the completion of the 3rd edition in 2000. Their letter captures the spirit of the document both then and now.

Best Regards,

Erica A. Miller, DVM

January 2012

February 2000

Fellow Wildlife Rehabilitators,

We are pleased to offer to you this revised and updated *Minimum Standards for Wildlife Rehabilitation*. This is a cooperative effort that represents the most current knowledge, expertise and techniques in our field. It is a reflection of what we have learned collectively, and have successfully applied during the last three decades. These *Minimum Standards* are based on accepted norms in biology, medicine, behavior, natural history, and, of course, wildlife rehabilitation. The information pertains to all who rehabilitate wildlife, regardless of numbers and types of wildlife cared for, budget size, number of paid or volunteer staff, and size and location of activity.

This book is a foundation upon which each wildlife rehabilitator can build an appropriate and effective practice. The goal is to give each animal the best chance of post-release survival in its natural place in the wild. Wildlife rehabilitators should combine information from *Minimum Standards*, current publications, wildlife veterinarians, experienced mentors, and personal experience, along with common sense and good judgment to make the best decisions for each individual animal. All rehabilitators are encouraged to improve upon these standards as they strive to provide the best possible care.

Although this edition is our current foundation, we recognize that as we learn more about housing sizes and materials, nutrition, species behavior, and other aspects of wildlife rehabilitation and medicine, we will certainly improve our methods. Future editions will incorporate the advancements we make.

This document has been designed BY wildlife rehabilitators FOR wildlife rehabilitators. We understand that some wildlife agencies have chosen to use all or parts of our *Minimum*

Standards in their permitting or licensing processes. We encourage such use but stress that the information must be kept in context and used to improve the rehabilitative care of wildlife. Our intent is not to exclude, but to include and encourage rehabilitators as they strive to improve.

Our Wildlife Rehabilitator's Code of Ethics is a part of these *Minimum Standards* and is based on the principles of honesty, integrity, responsibility, and treating others as we would have them treat us. The Code of Ethics provides basic rules of conduct for each of us to incorporate into our practice. The resulting self-respect, peer respect, and community respect and credibility will increase our effectiveness in animal care, networking, fund-raising, volunteer management, educational efforts, and all aspects of wildlife rehabilitation. Ethical and professional conduct by each wildlife rehabilitator will also contribute significantly to the credibility of our field as a whole, which, in turn, will benefit all of us.

We are proud of this collaborative effort! We encourage all wildlife rehabilitators to actively use this document to help improve the care, treatment, and successful release of wildlife.

Elaine M. Thrune, President
National Wildlife Rehabilitators Association

Marjorie Gibson, President
International Wildlife Rehabilitation Council

STATEMENT OF PURPOSE

The *Minimum Standards for Wildlife Rehabilitation* (*Minimum Standards*) is a document created by and for wildlife rehabilitators. This document is intended to help increase the number of rehabilitated wildlife that are successfully returned to wild populations by providing: a) standards and guidelines for care; b) a mechanism for self-evaluation; and c) recommendations and information regarding wildlife care. All rehabilitators and regulatory agencies are encouraged to explore and understand the principles underlying these standards, and to apply them in the everyday care of wild animals.

This document is not intended to be an enforcement program. Each region may or may not have its own requirements for rehabilitation activities and facilities. Permit requirements vary and are not necessarily related to this document. Some government agencies, however, use this document when establishing permit programs. The US Fish and Wildlife Service and a number of states use the caging dimensions contained in *Minimum Standards*, 3rd edition (2000) as guidelines for part of the requirements for rehabilitation permits for migratory birds and endangered species. (US Fish and Wildlife Service 50 CFR Parts 17, 21 and 22 RIN 1018–AH87; < http://policy.fws.gov/library/03-26823.pdf >).

The *Minimum Standards* is not a static textbook, but a living document that changes constantly as the field of wildlife rehabilitation grows and improves, and as the needs of individual animals demand. The procedures and cage sizes described herein have been developed by experienced wildlife rehabilitators, and are considered to be minimal — i.e., more detailed procedures or specialized cages are certainly acceptable and encouraged! Because wildlife patients undergoing rehabilitation are individuals, each with different injuries and unique behaviors, recommended cage sizes and techniques may not apply to every case. The wildlife rehabilitator is encouraged to alter techniques for housing, pre-release conditioning and other aspects of the rehabilitation process, so long as basic natural history, comfort, and hygiene needs are met. Cage dimensions can be modified to accommodate special needs of the facility, animal or new advancements in the field.

These *Minimum Standards* do NOT apply to animals kept beyond the normal scope of wildlife rehabilitation. Animals that are kept for educational, display, or captive breeding purposes have different housing requirements based on the long-term needs of the individual. Those specific needs are not addressed in this document. The book *Wildlife in Education: A Guide for the Care and Use of Program Animals* (Buhl and Borgia 2004) addresses housing, feeding, training, and safety requirements for animals that are used in on-site and off-site educational programs. This book does not address using animals in any static display environments or breeding programs.

Definitions of Commonly Used Terms

Animal: (Used as a general term in this text); individual of the mammalian, avian, reptilian, and/or amphibian classes.

Conspecifics: Individuals of the same species.

Euthanasia: The induction of death with minimal pain, stress, or anxiety; often the humane and appropriate option for nonreleasable wild animals suffering from incurable and/or painful injuries or disease.

Minimal: (adj.) Relating to or being a minimum; the least possible; barely adequate

Minimum: (noun; adj.) The least quantity asignable, admissible, possible.

Profession: The body of people in a learned occupation.

Standard: A reference point against which other things can be evaluated.

Stress: The sum of the biological reactions to any adverse stimulus, physical, mental, or emotional, internal or external, that tends to disturb an organism's homeostasis; the stimuli that elecit the reactions.

Wildlife Rehabilitation: The treatment and temporary care of injured, diseased, and displaced indigenous animals, and the subsequent release of healthy animals to appropriate habitats in the wild.

Wildlife Rehabilitation Facility or Center: A location at which wildlife rehabilitation is conducted, whether at an individual's home, a triage location, a facility dedicated to wildlife rehabilitation, or a place whose primary activity is not wildlife rehabilitation (such as a nature center, a domestic animal humane society, a veterinary clinic, or a university), but at which wildlife rehabilitation does occur.

Wildlife Rehabilitation Permit: A permit, license, or other written authorization issued by a federal, state, or provincial governmental agency authorizing the temporary possession of wildlife for the purpose of rehabilitation and eventual release back to the wild.

Wildlife Rehabilitator: A person who obtains or works under the current required government permits and pursues ongoing training and education to engage in the practice of wildlife rehabilitation.

Zoonoses: Diseases transmissible from non-human animals to humans (and vice-versa).

Chapter 1 – MINIMUM STANDARDS FOR REHABILITATION PROCESS

Minimum Standards for Wildlife Rehabilitation is a joint effort of the National Wildlife Rehabilitators Association (NWRA) and the International Wildlife Rehabilitation Council (IWRC). The objectives of this document are to establish professional standards for wildlife rehabilitation, to encourage the development of improved wildlife rehabilitation programs, and to improve care for all wild animals in rehabilitation.

Complying with *Minimum Standards* requires self-examination by the rehabilitator. Improvements in care and treatment protocols can be made and better facilities can be planned for using the information set forth in this publication. These minimum standards have been formulated by committee members, with extensive input from IWRC and NWRA members, and approved by the Boards of Directors of both of these wildlife rehabilitation organizations.

This document has been designed to accommodate both the individual rehabilitator and the rehabilitation organization.

1.1 Background

The need for minimum standards for wildlife rehabilitation became apparent about 25 years ago. Wildlife rehabilitation on the other hand, in one form or another, has existed for many years; it has ranged from the good-hearted individuals who first applied improvised methods for returning injured or orphaned wildlife to their native habitat, to the dedicated individuals and institutions that today continue this tradition with the increased knowledge, resources and support that results from decades of collective experience. Organized wildlife care programs originated as an outgrowth of nature and science centers and humane societies in response to public concern for injured wildlife. Some of these programs are now over fifty years old.

The field of wildlife rehabilitation experienced rapid growth beginning in the early 1970s as people became more environmentally aware of the limits of our natural resources. Oil spills triggered large scale attempts to save thousands of oiled water birds and helped raise the consciousness of industry, government and the public about the multiple hazards faced by wildlife. Programs were organized to address the impacts of human populations on native wildlife. Most of these efforts were accomplished with few funds, volunteer assistance, pre-existing facilities, and without government support.

In the early 1980s, financial support for these endeavors came mainly from private sources and, in a small part, from government sources. The numbers of paid staff positions began to increase as newly established organizations developed fund raising abilities and benefited from the support of the public. During the 1980s and 1990s, and into the current century, there has been an increase in the development of entirely new wildlife care facilities to improve those used in the 1970s.

Also in the early 1980s, before many states had regulations governing wildlife rehabilitation, the Boards of Directors of the NWRA and the IWRC saw a need to establish and expand basic minimum standards for both individual rehabilitators and rehabilitation centers. This was a method of self-regulation: making sure that rehabilitators knew what was acceptable, and making sure that rehabilitators knew what was necessary to provide quality care for the wildlife patients in their charge, a step deemed necessary in a field with rapidly chang-ing information and techniques. Both organizations formed "Standards Committees," and members from both committees worked together as a joint committee to develop these "Minimum Standards."

The result of these meetings was the first edition of *Minimum Standards for Wildlife Rehabilitation* (*Minimum Standards*), a 33-page booklet published by both organizations in 1989. The booklet offered rehabilitators a means of "self-regulating" when no other regula-tions were available. These "self-regulations" were written by rehabilitators and for rehabilitators.

In 1993, the Standards Committees from both IWRC and NWRA updated the *Minimum Standards* booklet based on feedback they had received from members of both organiza-tions. The changes were minor, and were done as an insert to the existing book, and later that year the changes were incorporated into a new printing of the booklet.

In 2000, with improved electronic communications (email), the members of both Standards Committees easily formed a joint committee and worked together to update the booklet once again. Requests for input were posted in the newsletters of both organizations, on their websites, and on various Internet list serves. Information was gathered from rehabilita-tors across the country and reviewed by committee members with expertise in the specific areas. The contributors and committee members agreed that the goal of the *Minimum Stan-dards* was to help all rehabilitators provide quality care to wildlife; it shouldn't matter if an injured creature is brought to a home-based rehabilitator or to a large rehabilitation center— the quality of care should be the same. With this in mind, this new edition was written so that it is applicable to all rehabilitators; the distinctions between "home-based" and "center" rehabilitation were removed. The resulting 75-page booklet, the 3rd edition of *Minimum Standards*, was published in 2000. Again, this booklet was written by and for rehabilitators, wishing to ensure the quality of care given to their wildlife charges.

In 2004, the joint Standards Committee undertook reviewing the 3rd edition of the *Minimum Standards* to make certain that the information was current and to incorporate additional information and suggestions that had been gathered from rehabilitators over the past four years. This project grew, and additional information was gathered through 2008. This 4th edition of the *Minimum Standards for Wildlife Rehabilitation* contains new information, in-cluding metric measurements for cages, an expanded section on reptile housing, flowcharts for dealing with infant wildlife, updated references, and a manufacturer list for products mentioned in this document.

The Standards Committee welcomes comments and suggestions for improving this docu-ment in future editions. Please address these ideas to both NWRA and IWRC using the contact information on the title page.

1.2 Minimum Care Requirements

This chapter walks the wildlife rehabilitator through a series of steps specifically designed to increase the chance of a successful release. The information in this first chapter will orient the rehabilitator to basic protocols and introduce her/him to the information in the following chapters.

The goal of this chapter is to provide a blueprint for successful rehabilitation and guide the rehabilitator through the basic care and clinical protocols. Examples of information forms are found in Appendix A. Using forms ensures that vital information is gathered for each patient. Written records are important in measuring how rehabilitation affects wildlife, therefore, a section describing statistical standards is also provided. Many rehabilitation permits require a cooperating veterinarian as a condition for legitimate operation of a wildlife care facility (of any size), and a veterinary policy is provided to clarify how this relationship is intended to work. Three facilities review checklists can be found in Appendix A: one is a useful self-evaluation tool compiled by the contributors to this book, one is a modified version of a checklist used by some agency personnel to determine if a facility meets their expectations, and the third is a checklist designed to be used by in-home rehabilitators.

Minimum standards for wildlife rehabilitation apply not only to the facilities used for rehabilitation, but to all aspects of the work involved. The outline in Table 1 is meant to serve both as guidance for the rehabilitator, and as an explanation of the rehabilitation process for the non-rehabilitator.

Various steps of the process will change from one patient to another, depending on the species, the condition of the individual animal, and other conditions specific to that case. In all cases, additional steps may certainly be added; however, the rehabilitator should try to include these basic steps for each patient. The order of the steps taken and the specifics involved in each step (for example, the type and quantity of fluids) will depend on each animal, its condition, and the materials and experience available to the rehabilitator. The initial treatment will vary the most, depending again on the nature of the injury, the individual animal, the overall condition of the animal, and the materials and experience available to the rehabilitator.

Table 1: Chronologic Outline of the Rehabilitation Process - Minimum Care Procedures for Wildlife Rehabilitation

1) Admission of the Animal
   a) Gather history from the person presenting the animal
   b) Record all information (Forms 4 & 5, Appendix A)
   c) Provide relevant educational material to the presenter
   d) For baby animals, determine if the animal is in need of rehabilitative care or could be placed back in its nest/den; if the latter, arrange return of the animal(s) accordingly (Charts 1 & 2, Appendix B)

2) Stabilization of the Animal
   a) Evaluate the animal quickly when transferring to a holding pen/cage/etc.
   b) Examine for critical conditions and administer emergency care as needed
   c) Provide warmth (unless hyperthermic)
   d) Provide quiet rest space
   e) Prepare materials needed for exam

Before handling the animal for the full exam, observe quietly for posture and behavior

3) Initial Examination
   a) Animal identification (species, age, gender if sexually dimorphic)
   b) Weight
   c) Temperature (as able)
   d) Visual exam
   e) Palpate limbs
   f) Examine orifices
   g) Assess nutritional status and condition

4) Initial Treatment
   a) Provide fluids
   b) Clean and treat any wounds
   c) Stabilize fractures
   d) Administer medications (antibiotics, analgesics, remedies, etc.)
   e) Provide appropriate, palatable nutrition for species and status
   f) Conduct or schedule any ancillary diagnostics (radiographs, bloodwork, fecals, etc.) and any additional treatments (surgeries, follow-up wrap changes, etc.)

5) Intensive Rehabilitation
   a) Monitor weight
   b) Provide ongoing, appropriate fluids and nutrition
   c) Treat medical problems as needed
   d) Provide comfortable, appropriate housing and habitat, minimize interaction with human activity

6) Intermediate Rehabilitation (restricted activity)
   a) Monitor weight
   b) Provide ongoing, appropriate nutrition
   c) Treat medical problems as needed (should be minimal)
   d) Provide comfortable, appropriate housing and habitat with mental stimulation, minimize interaction with human activity
   e) Provide manual physical therapy as needed
   f) Monitor behavior

7) Pre-Release Conditioning (unlimited activity)
   a) Provide larger, outdoor housing
   b) Monitor weight and general condition
   c) Provide ongoing, appropriate nutrition, introducing a more natural diet
   d) Treat any primary or secondary medical problems as needed (should be minimal)
   e) Exercise daily, as appropriate for that species

8) Release Evaluation (exceptions for some of the following items may occur when natural circumstances cannot be replicated in captivity)
   a) Ability to self-feed (perhaps catch live prey)
   b) Normal mobility and function, reasonable level of physical fitness and stamina necessary for foraging, breeding, migration, or territory defense behavior if predicted
   c) No evidence of disease
   d) Normal weight for that species/sex/season
   e) Normal blood values (where appropriate/feasible and known)
   f) Suitable release sites available (see Section 7.2)
   g) Normal behavior (the animal exhibits reasonable responses to human activity, exhibits normal socialization with both same and other species)

9) Release
   a) Provide proper/safe transportation
   b) Choose appropriate season/time of year (migration, breeding season, etc.)
   c) Choose appropriate time of day
   d) Provide food if appropriate
   e) Monitor post-release activity and behavior, if possible

1.3 Minimum Basic Knowledge for Wildlife Rehabilitators

Certain basic knowledge is needed before one can be an effective wildlife rehabilitator. In many cases, documentation of knowledge and/or training is required to obtain permits necessary to allow wildlife rehabilitation activities. In any case, acquiring knowledge before acquiring animals will enable the practitioner to provide better care for each animal.

Knowledge should be based on science and sound practice. Such knowledge can be acquired through a combination of academic instruction, on-the-job training, professional conferences and training seminars, and networking with colleagues. Much knowledge can be committed to memory, but the rehabilitator should have resources available at all times to access needed information.

Recommended Knowledge

- General knowledge should be acquired regarding wildlife rehabilitation.
- What is involved, including knowledge, training, legal requirements, cost, time commitment, emotional involvement, dangers, and rewards
- Regulations affecting wildlife rehabilitation, including state/provincial and federal wildlife rehabilitation regulations, health ordinances, zoning laws, etc.
- Ethics of wildlife rehabilitation
- Sources of information, training, references, networking, products, and materials
- Self-care recognition and methods to minimize stress and prevent burnout

More specific knowledge should be acquired pertaining to the species to be rehabilitated.
- Basic identification, including different ages
- Natural history and behavior
- Identification and general assessment of common wildlife problems and conditions
- Working with orphans, including imprinting, taming, and habituation
- Safe capture and handling, including restraint, transport, hygiene, and human vaccinations
- Wildlife parasites and diseases, including zoonoses
- Basic anatomy, examination procedure, and first aid
- Basic nutrition, dietary needs, and feeding techniques
- Working effectively with a cooperating veterinarian
- Facilities, housing/caging, and habitat needs
- Release criteria, considerations, and conditioning
- Euthanasia criteria and methods, including safe and legal disposal of materials and carcasses

Public information and education is a recognized part of wildlife rehabilitation and involves different knowledge than hands-on animal care.
- Effective communication techniques for handling phone calls and distributing information
- Humane solutions regarding human-wildlife conflicts, including preventing future problems
- When applicable, preparing and presenting effective public education programs

Acquiring Knowledge

Most wildlife rehabilitators acquire knowledge and training through a combination of reading, attending training seminars and conferences, volunteering or interning under the guidance of an experienced rehabilitator, and consulting with peers and mentors. College degrees are rarely available in wildlife rehabilitation and most schools do not offer classes in captive wildlife care. However, some colleges do offer classes in ornithology, mammalogy, animal behavior, ecology, and animal husbandry, and others offer courses for veterinary assistants and technicians. These college-level courses are not required, but may be starting points for wildlife rehabilitators to learn about animal nutrition, housing, handling, and general husbandry. Further study and experience can then assist in modifying and applying this basic information to the care of wild animals undergoing rehabilitation for the purpose of release.

General knowledge about wildlife rehabilitation can best be acquired by
- Reading *Principles of Wildlife Rehabilitation: The Essential Guide for Novice and Experienced Rehabilitators* (NWRA) and *Minimum Standards for Wildlife Rehabilitation* (NWRA/IWRC)
- Contacting the state wildlife agency office that governs wildlife rehabilitation activities for information on permit requirements, training, and nearby rehabilitators
- Contacting the USFWS for current information regarding federal permits required for avian and endangered species
- Visiting a rehabilitation center or individual licensed rehabilitator to learn more about what is involved in the work of rehabilitating wildlife

Knowledge specific to wildlife rehabilitation is available mainly through national and state/provincial wildlife rehabilitation associations and through training programs offered by wildlife rehabilitation centers. Gathering information requires resourcefulness, persistence, a willingness to purchase materials and attend seminars, and an ability to determine quality dependable information from inaccurate information. Various seminars, conferences, books, and journals are available through:
- National Wildlife Rehabilitators Association (< http://www.nwrawildlife.org >)
- International Wildlife Rehabilitation Council (< http://www.iwrc-online.org >)
- More than 25 state and provincial wildlife rehabilitation associations (list available on the NWRA website and in *Principles of Wildlife Rehabilitation*)
- Many wildlife rehabilitation centers and individually licensed rehabilitators accept volunteers and are willing to teach basic knowledge and skills. Locate these resources through wildlife rehabilitation association membership directories or by searching the NWRA *Training Opportunities in Wildlife Rehabilitation* on the NWRA website for job opportunities (both
- volunteer and paid).

Knowledge regarding informing and educating the public about wildlife and wildlife issues is available through:
- Presentations at national and state/provincial wildlife rehabilitation conferences
- *Principles of Wildlife Rehabilitation*
- *Wildlife in Education: A Guide for the Care and Use of Program Animals* (NWRA)
- *Introduction to Wildlife Education Programming: Tips and Techniques for Better Presentations* (NWRA)

- Positions listed in the *Training Opportunities in Wildlife Rehabilitation*
- National Association for Interpretation (NAI) (< http://www.interpnet.com >) and related state associations for environmental educators
- Conferences designed for naturalists and nature center educators

Acquiring the basic knowledge and an understanding of wildlife rehabilitation is a wise investment. It provides a sound basis for developing further knowledge and skills and enables the rehabilitator to provide high quality care for wildlife.

1.4 Recording & Reporting Requirements

Records are a vital part of any rehabilitation program, and are particularly important when an individual or an organization is trying to learn from previous work in an effort to improve the care given to wildlife. Record keeping has been placed in two categories: required information and recommended information. Records should be kept on all animals. Formats may vary. Records can be consolidated for healthy litters or clutches of animals raised for release. Daily forms for animals by pen, enclosure, or cage are required to verify that food, medications, and care are being provided.

Statistics should conform to specifications listed in Section 1.4. Annual statistics and, in some cases, individual case information are required to be reported to the US Fish and Wildlife Service and many state and provincial agencies. Individuals should check with their respective regulatory agencies to ensure that the correct information is being collected and submitted in the required format.

In addition, all birds (dead or alive) that indicate suspected poisoning or other criminal activity must be reported to the US Fish and Wildlife Service Law Enforcement Office immediately upon acquisition. All federal or state threatened or endangered species (dead or alive) and all bald or golden eagles must be reported to the permit-issuing office(s) within 48 hours.

Required Information

- Species
- Date admitted
- When and where found
- Name/address/phone number of finder
- Presenting injury/problem
- Initial weight
- Case or acquisition number
- Final disposition (i.e., released, transferred, placed, died, euthanized), including date, and location of release *where applicable*
- Recipient information if transferred or placed (name, address, permit number and purpose of transfer), including the transfer or placement of carcasses for educational purposes
- Type and amount of euthanasia drug if a controlled substance was used

- Federal band number, *where applicable*
- Completed daily care forms
- Record of notifying US Fish and Wildlife Service Regional Permit office in cases of endangered or threatened species, or bald or golden eagles
- Record of notifying US Fish and Wildlife Service Law Enforcement in cases of birds being shot, poisoned or victims of other illegal activity
- Any additional information required by state, provincial or federal permitting agencies

Recommended Information
- Any additional history that might be provided by the presenter (regarding cause of injury, severity or time of injury/problem, any care given by the presenter, etc.)
- Physical examination data
- Daily treatment information and efficacy
- Data regarding surgery, clinical pathology, necropsy, histopathology (where applicable)
- Release weight (if available; final weights may not be practical or prudent for high-stress animals or animals that are released via hacking)
- In cases of suspected poisoning or other illegal activity, any additional information describing the site where the animal was found, weather, other species present, relevant observations, etc.

See Appendix A for a sample form used to collect information from the person presenting the animal (form 2), and a sample examination form for collection of the other data (form 3). The sample forms were designed for use with birds, but could be easily adapted for use with other wildlife. See Appendix A form 6 for the collection and reporting of data relating to suspected poisoning or other illegal activity.

1.5 Statistical Standards

Definition of Disposition Codes

The code letters used by wildlife rehabilitators and rehabilitation centers can vary, but should be strictly defined for comparison purposes. All rehabilitators should use the main code categories (R, T, P, D, and E), while the subcategories are optional depending on the extend of detail desired by an individual or organization. Referenced categories should be broken down to meet the needs of the individual rehabilitator or center. Depending on the information that is desired, more detailed codes can be used. Detailed information later may be used to assess current treatment protocols, euthanasia guidelines, and totals of overall animals presented to a wildlife rehabilitator. This information may be useful for providing information to a presenter when he/she calls back to inquire about the animal they found; it may also be important when justifying budgets or volunteer staff needs at a facility. Referenced categories should correspond to the following:

R   (RELEASED): Any healthy, recovered animal returned to its natural, wild habitat after care. For individual center's information, this can be further subdivided into (optional):

> RTW (RETURNED TO WILD): Healthy animals sent back with the presenter to be released where found, to be put back into the nest, or to be reunited with the parents. Examples include healthy turtles "found" by children, and healthy nestlings and fledglings or cottontails returned to the nest site.

> RF (RETURNED, FOSTERED): Infant or juvenile animal fostered to adults of the same species—but not their actual parents—in the wild. Examples include Canada goslings introduced to a new family of Canada geese, raptor nestling placed into a new nest, and fawn introduced to a new doe.

T   (TRANSFERRED):

1) Any animal transported to another facility or wildlife rehabilitator for further rehabilitation efforts. (**Note: if the animal is known to have been released by the receiving facility, it is recorded as 'T' by the original facility and as 'R' by the receiving facility**).

2) Any animal determined to be non-releasable while undergoing wildlife rehabilitation efforts that is placed in a non-rehabilitation situation.

Note: Agency permission (federal and state or provincial) is usually required prior to transfer of live animals, and the recipient must possess the proper permits.

For individual center's information, this can be further subdivided into (optional):

> TR (TRANSFERRED FOR REHABILITATION OR CONTINUED CARE)
> TD (TRANSFERRED FOR DISPLAY)
> TE (TRANSFERRED FOR EDUCATIONAL PROGRAM)
> TPC (TRANSFERRED TO PERMANENT COLLECTION): Animal is being kept as part of *your organization's* display exhibits, for use in educational programs, for use as a surrogate, or for other permitted use of wildlife.

P   (PENDING): Any animal still undergoing rehabilitation efforts at the time that annual reports are due. These animals are only added to summary statistics after final resolution.

D   (DIED): Any animal either received dead or which dies during the rehabilitation process. Can be subdivided into (optional):

> DOA (DEAD ON ARRIVAL): Any animal that dies before any lifesaving measures or treatments can be implemented in the care facility.

> DBE (DIED BEFORE EXAMINATION): Any animal that was presented live but then died before it was examined. This assumes needed measures are undertaken immediately upon receiving the animal. Placing the animal in a quiet, dark environment is using a form of treatment.

D24H: Any animal that died within 24 hours of arrival. This death may be from the presenting injury/illness, handling, exam, treatment, or implementation of lifesaving measures in the care facility.

DIC (DIED IN CARE): Any animal that dies subsequent to the presenting injury/illness, or as a result of any handling, exam, treatment, or implementation of lifesaving measures in the care facility.

E   (EUTHANIZED): Any animal that is suffering or non-releasable that is euthanized. Can be subdivided into (optional):

EOA (EUTHANIZED ON ARRIVAL): Any animal euthanized after an initial exam without further treatment measures being done.

EIC (EUTHANIZED IN CARE): Any animal euthanized after treatment measures have been implemented.

AFE (ACCEPTED FOR EUTHANASIA): Animal was accepted for euthansia due to the center's policy on the species presented, state regulations, etc. Examples may include non-native species (European starlings, English sparrows, pigeons, etc.) and rabies vector species (RVS) such as bats, skunks, and raccoons.

Data Analysis for Release Rate for Releasable Animals

$$\% \text{ Released} = \frac{\# \text{ Released}}{(\text{Total} \# \text{ Received} - \text{DOA})}$$

Note: released animals do NOT include transferred, placed, or pending animals.

Rehabilitators are encouraged to divide their statistics further into the categories of avian, mammalian, and herpetile species, both for their own information, and to help with comparisons to data from other individuals and centers. This will help with statistical comparisons between those that deal strictly with avian species, those that deal with both avian and mammalian species, those that may deal strictly with herpetiles, etc. Many rehabilitators also calculate their release rate by subtracting the EOA, AFE, and DBE numbers from the Total Number Received in order to provide a more accurate view of those patients actually treated.

1.6 Veterinary Policy

In most states and under most circumstances, the legal prescription of medical care for wildlife patients is the responsibility of a veterinarian. The veterinarian may delegate a portion of this responsibility to a rehabilitator by means of a mutually agreeable, written protocol wherein these responsibilities are clearly defined, and the veterinarian should provide appropriate training to the rehabilitator to carry out these responsibilities. Such an arrangement allows the veterinarian to prescribe a specific treatment protocol for a specific type of injury without having to see each individual patient (e.g., the veterinarian may prescribe a certain antibiotic to be given at a specific dosage, frequency, and duration for all cat attack victims). Likewise, the veterinarian should rely on the rehabilitator to best address the husbandry needs of the animal (i.e., diet, housing, etc.). This agreement should provide a clear mutual understanding of the division of responsibilities consistent with state or provincial laws regarding the practice of veterinary medicine. This type of arrangement also requires that an appropriate veterinarian-rehabilitator-wildlife patient relationship exists and has the following components:

1. The veterinarian has sufficient knowledge of wildlife medicine to permit a general or preliminary diagnosis. This knowledge may be obtained from various sources including prior experience or specific wildlife-related training, the completion of continuing education courses related to wildlife species, consultation with wildlife veterinarians, as well as medical references specific to wildlife care.

2. Furthermore, the veterinarian has recently seen and is acquainted with the general conditions and care of the wildlife patients through medically appropriate and timely visits to the premises where the wildlife patients are kept, or timely transport of wildlife patients to the facility of the attending veterinarian.

3. The veterinarian has assumed the responsibility for any medical judgments regarding the health of wildlife patients and the need for medical treatments.

4. If the veterinarian intends to keep and treat any animal for more than 24 hours, the veterinarian must have the appropriate wildlife rehabilitation permit(s) or be listed as a sub-permittee to a wildlife rehabilitator. Wildlife housed at a veterinary hospital must be housed in an area that is quiet and removed from domestic animals and human traffic.

5. The veterinarian is available for follow-up in case of adverse reactions or failure of the regimen of therapy. Such follow-up should be specific in any written agreement between the rehabilitator and the veterinarian.

6. Any agreement must abide by the laws and regulations governing the practice of veterinary medicine where and if they apply to wildlife rehabilitation.

1.7 Wildlife Rehabilitation Facilities Review

Rehabilitation facilities and individual rehabilitators often benefit from doing a regular self-evaluation or self-review. Forms used to assist in this type of self-evaluation are found in Appendix A (Forms 1, 2, and 3). The purpose of these forms is to provide wildlife caregivers suggestions to save time (for example, keeping reference materials at the phone), to ensure wildlife receives appropriate housing and medical treatment (exam area, caging, veterinary and diagnostic), and to protect both wildlife and humans from disease and contamination (food preparation, disinfecting, housekeeping). Not all items contained in each form will apply to everyone—but these forms do provide an easy reference to be sure important considerations are not overlooked, especially when changes occur such as facility growth or unexpected species or numbers are admitted.

Chapter 2 – DISEASE CONTROL

2.1 Rationale for Disease Control

The safety and health of the humans caring for wildlife is a critical facet of successful rehabilitation. Many diseases are transmitted from animals to humans, and also from animal to animal. This chapter instructs rehabilitators on effective ways to prevent the spread of disease from wildlife to caretakers, domestic animals, and other wildlife patients. Proper disease control is a serious concern for rehabilitators and permit granting agencies. Adherence to the suggested protocols is highly recommended by the NWRA and the IWRC.

Facility cleanliness is an integral part of disease prevention and containment. Proper cleaning agents combined with a sensible cleaning schedule will reduce the spread of disease within a facility. Cleaning protocols vary considerably based on the species and condition of animals in care, facility type, and cage construction. Choice of cleaning agent must be made with these variables in mind. Included in this chapter are cleaning agent descriptions and a table of agent properties that will help in making appropriate selections. The timing of cleaning efforts is another important feature of effective disease prevention. Suggestions for proper and regular maintenance in this chapter will help rehabilitators prevent disease within their facility.

2.2 Prevention of Disease Transmission

Since transmissible diseases are so diverse in their origin and action, it is most useful to approach their control according to their mode of transmission. The general modes of transmission are:

1. Diseases passing directly from one vertebrate host to another via direct contact (bite, etc.)
2. Indirect transmission involving one or more intermediate hosts (vectors) such as arthropods or prey species
3. Indirect transmission involving aerosol particles or fomites (inanimate objects such as shoes, clothing, utensils, feeding tubes, food dishes, cage bedding, etc.)

Disease organisms enter the body by one or more of six routes:

1. Inhalation
2. Ingestion
3. Inoculation (animal bite, injection, insect bite, or direct contact via a pre-existing opening in the skin)
4. Genital tract via coitus or contaminated instruments
5. Transplacental (from the mother - mammals only)
6. Across the umbilicus or yolk (from the mother)

For each of these modes of transmission there must be an effective strategy to interrupt the transmission cycle. The wildlife rehabilitator's primary defense against diseases communicable from animal to humans is a high standard of personal hygiene. The primary control of diseases communicable from animal to animal is containment, with the first line of defense being the individual cage or pen.

2.3 Standards to Prevent Disease Transmission within the Facility

2.3.1 Control of Diseases Transmissible from Animals to Humans

- Clothing should be clean and changed as often as necessary. It is suggested that the facility provide lab coats or other tops to volunteers and launder them on-site.

- Shoes and boots should be kept clean of fecal matter, dirt, and cage litter.

- Disposable gloves and surgical masks must be available for use during such procedures as necropsies or cleaning contaminated animal quarters. Necropsy procedures must adhere strictly to sanitary practices including the use of surgical masks and disposable gloves, appropriate outer garments, and the use of disinfectants.

- Lavatory facilities should be accessible with hand-washing sinks and suitable washing agents.

- Eating, drinking and smoking should be restricted to designated areas free of animal waste materials.

- The supervisory staff must be given basic information on zoonoses. Personal hygiene rules should be established and the supervisory staff should set an example.

- All personnel and volunteers should be advised to seek the consent of their physicians before working in the facility. They should acquire any necessary vaccinations (especially tetanus). If working with mammals, they should inquire about the possibility of pre-exposure rabies vaccinations. Female workers who become pregnant should be advised to renew medical consent. Rehabilitators handling potential Rabies Vector Species (RVS—most adult mammals) should have pre-exposure rabies vaccinations. See Section 2.3.3.

- There must be separate refrigeration facilities for food (animal food kept separate from human food) and for carcasses and postmortem specimens.

2.3.2 Control of Diseases Transmissible from Animal to Animal

- Cages should be designed for efficient cleaning. When possible, seamless, nonporous materials (such as stainless steel, fiberglass or plastics) should be employed for cage construction and food containers.

- Animal enclosures should be kept sanitary by having an adequate and routine cleaning regimen in which responsibilities are clearly defined and assigned to personnel. While daily removal of feces and urine from mammal cages is necessary to prevent odor, parasite re-infestation, and insect overpopulation, avian, reptile, and amphibian cages usually require less frequent cleaning. Many adult birds, especially songbirds, as well as other injured wildlife, are very easily stressed during the rehabilitation process, thus daily disturbances should be minimized. Any animal in contact with the cage substrate (e.g., infants, animals that are non-ambulatory due to illness or injury) will need to have the bedding or cage substrate changed more frequently than those animals who can perch or ambulate well within the cage. Infant mammal and bird caging requires much more frequent cleaning because infants tend to have limited movement and soil their nests repeatedly through the day: bedding or nest cup linings should be changed each time the animals are fed. The floors of many indoor avian cages may be lined with layers of newspaper, paper towels, or other substrates, which can be removed one layer at a time for easy disposal of urates, feces, etc. Large flight aviaries also may be cleaned on a less frequent basis, provided there is a regular schedule for cleaning. Caging for aquatic herpetiles may be kept clean primarily through the use of proper water filtration systems. If a water filtration system is unavailable, the water *must* be changed several times daily and immediately each time the water becomes contaminated with feces.

- Indoor facilities are required to have efficient ventilation and air movement with minimal recycled or reused air.

- In all circumstances, protocols for regular cleaning should be in place, and all cages and cage furnishings should be properly disinfected between patients (when an animal or group of animals is removed, the cage should be disinfected before new animals are placed in the cage). Because of the high incidence of *Baylisascaris procyonis* (the intestinal roundworm of raccoons), the fatal transmission of this parasite to other species, and the high resistance of this parasite to disinfectants, caging used for raccoons should be designated as such, and should not be used to house other species. Before a newly-acquired animal is introduced into a cage or enclosure that has previously been used by another animal, the cage must be thoroughly cleaned and disinfected and the bedding material changed.

- Animals confirmed or suspected of having contagious diseases must be kept isolated in a separate room from all noninfected susceptible animals. Newly acquired animals should be housed separately from in-house animals upon arrival. Animals that are presented together (littermates or nestmates) may be housed together during this period. They should not be added to a group pen until it has been established that they are in good health.

- A routine examination for parasites should be performed on new arrivals, with re-examination at intervals during protracted rehabilitation.

- Bowls, feeding utensils, medical equipment, linens used for handling animals and for animal bedding, and gloves worn while handling wildlife should also be cleaned/replaced daily and disinfected between use on different animals.

- Water bowls should be cleaned and/or changed as needed to keep them clear of algae, leaves, feces, and other debris.

- Outdoor water sources should be cleaned a minimum of twice weekly to prevent mosquitos from reproducing in them.

- Animal diets must be prepared and foodstuffs should be stored under sanitary conditions that ensure freedom from vermin and microbial contamination.

2.3.3 Public Health Responsibilities

- All organic refuse must be collected into airtight bags or containers and stored in a safe location until it is removed from the premises. The supervisory staff is responsible to local public health officials on matters regarding waste and postmortem material disposal.

- All staff and volunteers should receive thorough training regarding health and safety concerns relating to both zoonotic diseases and potential physical hazards of handling wildlife.

- Domestic animals should not be allowed at the rehabilitation facility. If this is un-avoidable, domestic animals should be fully vaccinated and should have no direct contact with, nor direct exposure to, wildlife.

- Untrained personnel (i.e., non-staff or volunteers) should not have access to wildlife holding areas. Public access should be limited to display (non-releasable) animals, and all tours should be escorted by trained personnel and should not include any contact with the animals in care.

- Personnel must take care to properly wash and change clothes before coming in contact with domestic animals.

- A program for rodent and insect control is recommended for wildlife care facilities; however, if pesticides are used, care should be taken to avoid contaminating both human and animal food and housing areas with pesticides.

- The rescuer or individual presenting an animal to a rehabilitator should be questioned regarding the possibility of any contact with the animal, such as bites or scratches. If injured, the individual should immediately be referred to his/her own physician for medical attention. The rehabilitator should also notify the public health department of any such injuries, if required by state law. If the bite or injury is from an RVS, the animal should be euthanized and tested for rabies.

- All rehabilitators, volunteers, and transporters handling mammals (especially adults) should have pre-exposure rabies vaccinations and be knowledgeable in the handling of these species and have thorough RVS safety training. Any bites from an RVS should be reported to the public health department, and the rehabilitators should consult their state public health lab regarding testing the animal for rabies. Some health departments may prefer to receive the entire animal carcass, whereas others may prefer to receive only the head; furthermore, some may arrange to pick up the specimen while others require delivery to them. Animals that are to be tested should be refrigerated immediately following death or euthanasia. Some laboratories may be able to test specimens that have been frozen once, but many cannot; always consult your local laboratory prior to freezing a rabies suspect carcass (Appendix A Form 7 - Sample Rabies Submission form).

- Since rabies vector species often do not exhibit obvious clinical signs and since nonbite rabies transmission is possible, every wildlife rehabilitator in rabies endemic areas must decide on a safe and humane policy towards these species. State wild-life agencies and public health departments should be consulted and their regulations should be respected. Safety and health training should be available for all persons handling rabies vector species. Access to wildlife in holding areas should be restricted to prevent unnecessary contact and exposures.

2.3.4 Release Considerations

Rehabilitated adult mammals should be released within the animal's normal home range, or no more than 10 miles from point of capture, when possible and reasonable. This practice minimizes the unnatural spread of parasites, diseases, and genetic material among wild populations, and maximizes the animal's chance of survival. Exact release location and time should be chosen at the discretion of the rehabilitator, based on the appropriateness of the habitat and the condition of the animal, as well as state or local regulations regarding the translocation of wildlife. When circumstances allow, rehabilitated adult birds should be released in a suitable habitat as close as possible to the point of their capture except during migration. If migration has occurred while the bird has been in captivity, the bird should be released in the area of the migratory destination. Studies have shown that rehabilitated reptiles and amphibians should be released within 1/2 mile of the point of capture to maximize their chance of survival.

If information regarding the location of capture is not available, the release of the animal should be within the standards set by the state/provincial wildlife agency and should meet all habitat requirements of the animal. Intimate knowledge of both the species' and the individual's natural history and behavioral patterns is essential in choosing the correct habitat. Studies that examine outcomes of released animals indicate that incorrect habitat selection increases mortality.

Juvenile animals, especially those that were brought into rehabilitation as infants, do not have to be released at the site of capture to ensure survival; however, efforts still should be made to release these animals within 10 miles of the capture site, if possible. When return is not possible (retrieval area is contaminated, contains definite hazards for the animal or the individual doing the release, etc.), these animals should be released in a suitable habitat.

Some considerations when assessing what a suitable habitat constitutes for a particular species include: adequate space not occupied by territorial conspecifics; suitable shelter; proper terrain and vegetation; good food and water supply; minimal number of predators; and suitable distance from human development.

2.3.5 Disposal of Carcasses and Animal Waste Products

Each animal that dies or is euthanized while under the care of a wildlife rehabilitator should always be examined carefully to confirm that the animal really is dead (lack of pulse or heart beat). Carcasses should then be disposed of properly and in accordance with local laws and parameters set forth in individual wildlife rehabilitation permits (e.g., the rehabilitator may be required to transfer the carcasses of endangered species to a specified location). Unless otherwise directed, all bald and golden eagle carcasses and loose feathers must be sent to the National Eagle and Wildlife Property Repository (Rocky Mountain Arsenal, Building 128, Commerce City, Colorado 80022, PH: 303-287-2110).

If the rehabilitator plans to necropsy the carcass or transfer it to a diagnostic facility for the purpose of necropsy, the carcass should be wet with cold water, unless the animal is a suspected victim of pesticide poisoning (water might remove pesticides contaminating the outside of the animal). The addition of a small amount of detergent to the water will help to penetrate the fur or feathers, speeding up the process of cooling the body. If the necropsy is not performed immediately, the wet carcass should be placed in a plastic bag, sealed, labeled, and refrigerated in an ice chest or refrigerator not used for food storage. A necropsy performed shortly after death allows collection of more accurate information. This accuracy fades as more time passes due to postmortem changes that can alter or mask signs. Gloves and surgical mask must be worn while conducting necropsies. Necropsies should be performed in a well-ventilated location, separate from live animal and food preparation areas.

Note: Endangered or threatened species and bald or golden eagles must not be necropsied without first obtaining permission from the US Fish and Wildlife Service.

Carcasses that are not necropsied may be transferred to approved natural history museums, universities or other institutions for study and/or addition to their collections. The wildlife rehabilitator should contact these institutions and arrange for proper handling of the carcasses so that the institutions can gain the most benefit from them (e.g., carcasses may need to be frozen, placed in formalin, etc.). Specific data also may need to be recorded by the rehabilitator such as date and location animal was found, live body weight, etc. In many cases, the information provided by the rehabilitator can be as valuable as the specimen itself.

If the wildlife rehabilitator desires to keep specific parts or portions of avian carcasses (e.g., skeletons or skins for educational purposes, etc.), special permits first must be obtained from the US Fish and Wildlife Service. Many state wildlife agencies also require special permits to possess wildlife parts. Special permits are not required for the rehabilitator to possess a limited number of feathers (excluding eagle feathers) for imping purposes.

All other carcasses and all animal waste products should be disposed of in accordance with acceptable practices as required by local ordinances as well as applicable state/provincial and federal regulations. Carcasses and organic wastes suspected of disease contamination

either should be buried or incinerated. Where legal, burial of carcasses should be at a depth that will discourage scavenger species from unearthing them, and lime should be spread on top of the carcasses to assist in disease control. Incinerators are generally cost prohibitive to most rehabilitators and rehabilitation facilities, and special permits are required to operate incinerators in most areas. Many local animal control shelters or laboratories have incinerators and the rehabilitator may be able to arrange for these facilities to incinerate carcasses on a regular basis. Carcasses may be frozen for a limited period of time (in nonfood freezers) for storage prior to incineration or donation to pre-approved facilities (public institutions or individuals authorized to possess the specimens for educational purposes).

2.4 Disinfection

Disease control and prevention (section 2.3) are the obvious "why's" of facility cleanliness. The following information pertains to the "how's" of creating and maintaining a clean facility.

2.4.1 Definition of Common Terms

Antiseptic:
A substance capable of preventing infection by inhibiting the growth of infectious agents (implies use on living tissue).

Bacterial spores:
The resting or vegetative stage of certain bacteria (especially *Bacillus* and *Clostridium*) characteristically very resistant to environmental changes.

Cytotoxic:
Having the characteristic of killing cells.

Diluent:
Substance used to make a concentrated solution more dilute. Sterile water and saline are common diluents for wound treatment, and tap water is a common diluent for general disinfection.

Disinfectant:
A substance that destroys microbial organisms or inhibits their activity.

Disinfection:
Destruction of vegetative forms of microorganisms (implies use on inanimate objects).

Sterilization:
The destruction of all microorganisms in or about an object (term is only used with inanimate objects). [Note: "cold sterilization" refers to the specific method of using a disinfectant solution to soak objects, rather than applying heat, pressure, or gas as used in other methods of sterilization].

Volatiles:
Agents that evaporate rapidly and pass readily in the form of a vapor. Toxic components within these vapors can be dangerous.

2.4.2 Types of Cleaning Agents

There are various disinfecting agents that should be used after regular cleaning to properly sanitize. Many of these disinfecants are inactivated by organic matter (dirt, feces, food, etc.), so proper cleaning should always precede disinfection. Suggested uses are listed under each category of cleaning agent, and some products work better against specific disease entities. The rehabilitator, however, should be aware that none of these products is designed for any specific target or single use. In addition, none of these products is specifically effective against nematode eggs or larvae (intestinal worms). Most parasites are best removed from the environment by simple mechanical means (i.e., removal of feces and physical scrubbing of cages and cage contents), while other parasites, such as *Baylisascaris spp.* and *Coccidia spp*, may be very difficult to completely remove from the environment. Many disinfectants emit potentially harmful volatiles; therefore, when disinfectants are used in cages, the cages should be allowed to dry thoroughly before placing animals into them. Some of the more common agents and methods are discussed here; additional information can be found in the references in Appendices C & E.

Detergents:
Detergents are cleaning compounds and include both soaps (anionic - alkali salts; negatively charged) and synthetic detergents (cationic - colloidal in solution; used as antiseptics, wetting agents, and emulsifiers; positively charged). While most soaps are non-antibacterial, the physical scrubbing action of cleaning removes many of the microorganisms. Detergents alone do have minor disinfectant action against vegetative bacteria; however, they are not effective against fungi or viruses. Additionally, they lose their effectiveness in the presence of blood or tissue debris.
Examples: Dish detergents and laundry detergents.
Uses: Initial washing of cages, food bowls, etc., to remove fecal, food, and other organic matter.

Alcohols:
Solutions of 50-70% isopropyl alcohol or 70% ethyl alcohol are commonly used alone or combined with other disinfectants. Isopropyl has a wider range of antibacterial action and is less corrosive than ethyl alcohol. Alcohols act by denaturing soluble proteins, interrupting metabolism, depressing surface tension and lysing (breaking open) cells. Because it is cytotoxic, alcohol should not be used on open wounds. Alcohols inactivate phenols, so the two should not be combined. Alcohols are not effective for cold sterilization, and may damage rubber, plastic and other synthetic materials.
Example: Rubbing alcohol.
Uses: surgical preparation, antiseptic, instruments.
Recommended dilution ratio: Use undiluted (i.e., 50-70%).

Aldehydes:
 The two most common disinfectants in this group are gluteraldehydes and formaldehyde. Gluteraldehydes are often combined with a synthetic detergent. These substances are irritating and cytotoxic, so their use is limited to disinfection, and instruments should be rinsed well before use. Exposure of 3 hours is required to kill bacterial spores. Formaldehyde is considered a carcinogen.
Examples: Wavicide™, Cidex™.
Uses: Glutaraldehydes may be used for cold pack sterilization, disinfection; formalin (40% formaldehyde in water) may be used to fumigate premises.
Recommended dilution ratio: Use gluteraldehydes undiluted (i.e., 2.0%) for disinfection; use formalin at 1-10% for fumigation.

Chlorhexidine:
This bisbiguanide compound acts on bacterial cell membranes, precipitates intracellular contents, and inhibits ATP (adenosine triphosphate, an energy source for cells--in this case the energy source of the bacteria). The cell membrane damage causes leakage of potassium and pentoses, which kills the bacteria, but also harms host cells. Can dilute in water or saline. The brand name Virosan™ contains alcohol, making it effective against pseudomonads; however, once mixed with water this solution is only effective for 3-4 days.
Example: Nolvasan™ (2%), Virosan™.
Uses: Surgical preparation, wound treatment, disinfection.
Recommended dilution ratio: 1 ml chlorhexidine + 39 ml diluent (0.5%) for wounds, and1ml chlorhexidine + 19 ml diluent (1.0%) for disinfection.

Chlorine:
Chlorine-based products are oxidizers, releasing free radicals that destroy cells. These compounds indiscriminately attack microorganisms, organic matter and living tissue. Higher concentrations (more free chlorine) are needed to kill viruses and when organic matter is present. Chlorine decomposes in the presence of light and has toxic fumes that can lead to chemical pneumonia and skin and eye burns. Good ventilation, eye protection and gloves are recommended when using Chlorines.
Examples: Clorox Bleach™, Purex™ (should be 5.25% sodium hypochlorite).
Uses: Disinfection of nonmetallic objects and surfaces.
Recommended dilution ratio: 1:32 (1/2 cup of 5.25% bleach per gallon hot water) for all-purpose disinfectant use; 1:20 (6.5 oz of 5.25% bleach per gallon hot water).

<u>Stabilized Chlorine Dioxides:</u>
Stabilized chlorine dioxide is an inorganic compound of oxygen and chlorine and is a powerful oxidizing agent. Chlorine dioxides stimulate an oxidation process that safely breaks and eliminates sulfur bonds responsible for organic odor. Can be safely used around birds. It will clean and provide disinfectant protection and is not harmful. For hard surfaces, the solution is sprayed on and then wiped off after a 5 minute exposure. Rinsing is not necessary. Oxyfresh Dent-a-gene™ is a full strength stabilized chlorine dioxide disinfectant that is a two-part product. The two parts are mixed (at this stage it does have toxic fumes) but once stabilized it is safe for use. A mixed solution can be used for 7 days if sealed tightly and kept out of the light.
Examples: Bio-Rite™, DioxiCare™, Oxyfresh Dent-a-gene™, Oxyfresh Cleansing Gele™, Oxine©
Uses: Washing/soaking solution for syringes, food dishes, feeders and water containers; general disinfection of premises.
Recommended dilution ratio: Varies with product, follow label directions.

<u>Cresols:</u>
Cresols are wood tar distillates that have solvent and antibacterial properties. Commercial cresols available as disinfectants usually consist of pine oils combined with soap. These substances are often difficult to remove from surfaces and may leave a slick coating to floors or other surfaces.
Examples: Hexol™, Pine-Sol™.
Uses: Disinfection of premises.
Recommended dilution ratio: None listed in literature.

<u>Iodophores:</u>
These compounds consist of iodine complexed with surfactants or polymers. The most common compound is povidone iodine (iodine + polyvinylpyrrolidone), available as a solution and as a scrub. The detergent used in the scrub form is cytotoxic and should not be used on open wounds. The polyvinylpyrrolidone has a high affinity for cell membranes, delivering the iodine more directly to the target cells (e.g., bacteria), but it is the free iodine that contains the disinfectant action; therefore, dilutions of povidone iodine actually disinfect or kill infectious agents better than more concentrated solutions. Iodine kills bacterial spores if contact time is greater than 15 minutes.
Example: Betadine™ Solution and Betadine™ Scrub (10%).
Uses: Surgical preparation, wound treatment, hand cleansers, foot baths, disinfection.
Recommended dilution ratio: 1 ml povidone-iodine + 99 ml diluent (0.1%) for surgical preparation and 1ml povidone-iodine + 9 ml diluent (1.0%) for wound treatment.

<u>Phenols:</u>
Phenols are cytotoxic by disrupting cell walls and precipitating cellular proteins. Some phenols have been shown to cause neurotoxicity and teratogenicity (birth defects) after long dermal exposure, so animals should be removed from the quarters during cleaning; the use of goggles and gloves is recommended. Phenols are extremely toxic to cats and may be toxic to reptiles.
Examples: Avinol-3™, Lysol™, One Stroke Environ™.
Uses: General disinfection, foot baths.
Recommended dilution ratio: 1/2 oz One Stroke per gallon diluent.

Quaternary Ammonium Compounds (QAC):
QAC's are a form of cationic detergent, but they are not compatible with other soaps or detergents, and even the residues of these substances and/or organic matter will inactivate QAC's. Activity is increased, however, by the addition of ethanol. These compounds act by direct denaturation of bacterial enzyme systems and neutralization of acidic elements in the bacterial cell walls.
Examples: Kennel Kare™, Kennelsol™, Parvosol™, Quinticare™, Roccal D™.
Uses: Some wound treatment, general disinfection.
Recommended dilution ratio: 1 part QAC to 2,500 parts diluent for wounds; 1 part QAC to 200 parts diluent for disinfection.

General Comment on Potential Environmental Toxins:
Many disinfectants and their fumes, especially at full-strength, may cause skin, eye and lung irritation, and may be toxic if ingested. Care should be taken to wear gloves while using these products, and to work in a well-ventilated area. Most chemical compounds, including disinfectants, some cleansers and even some drugs, must be accompanied by a material safety data sheet (MSDS) explaining the potential health hazards and how to prevent or treat exposure. These information sheets are usually packaged with the products or can be obtained from the manufacturer. The Occupational Safety and Health Administration (OSHA), as well as most insurance companies, require that a complete file of appropriate MSDS's be kept on scene and readily available/accessible to all employees and volunteers.

In addition to human safety, care must be taken to prevent chemical exposure to wildlife. Animals should be kept away from all volatile chemicals at all times. This includes phenols, ammonia, bleach, and most common household cleansers. If these cleansers must be used, the animals must be removed from the room they are being used in until it has thoroughly aired. If any of these chemicals are used to disinfect cages, they must be thoroughly rinsed and air-dried to prevent toxin accumulation. Cigarette should not be smoked near animals, particularly amphibians. Note that many pesticides will cause severe illness or even death in many birds, reptiles and nearly all amphibians.

2.4.3 Basic Cleaning Techniques

Ideally, all organic matter should be removed before it dries; however, this is not always practical. Once an area has been soiled and dried, it should be kept dry until the debris and waste can be removed. It is always better to sweep/pick up dry debris before applying chemicals and water. Dried, crusty, caked on waste or debris can be removed by scraping. Whatever is resistant to dry removal can then be soaked with an appropriate detergent solution to loosen or dissolve it for removal by an absorptive substance such as paper or cloth towels, newspaper, or other absorbants such as kitty litter. Some bodily waste substances can neutralize certain disinfectants, so all organic matter should be removed as completely as possible, including the complete removal of soaps or detergents, before applying disinfectants. Workers should take precautions to protect themselves, as well as other humans or animals in the area, from harmful gasses which may be emitted from some cleaners (e.g., ammonia or bleach). Goggles, gloves, and face masks, as well as protective clothing (long pants and sleeves, closed-toed shoes) should be worn as recommended on the disinfectant label. Once all solid matter has been removed and any liquified waste absorbed, the appropriate disinfection agent and methods should be used following an approved protocol.

Table 2: Properties of Disinfectants

Property or Spectrum of Action	Phenol	QAC	Cresol	Alcohol	odo-phore	Chlor-ine	Alde-hyde	Chlor-hexi-dine	Chlor-ine dioxide
GM+ bacteria	high	high	high	high	high	high	high	high	high
GM- bacteria	high	high	high	high	high	high	high	mod*	high
Bacterial spore	none	none	none	none	mod	none	mod	none	mod
Chlamydia	none	high	none	none	?	low	?	none	?
Fungi & yeasts	low	mod	mod	mod	high	high	high	mod	high
Viruses	mod	var	mod	mod	mod	high	high	mod	high
Protozoa	low	mod	?	mod	high	none	?	low	high
Effectiveness w/organic matter	mod	low	mod	none	mod	none	var	mod	low
Residual action	high	high	high	none	low	none	low	high	low
Effectiveness in hard water	var	low	var	NA	high	high	high	none	?
Most effective PH range	acid	alk	acid	NA	acid/alk	acid	acid	alk	?
Corrosiveness	high	none	mod	low	mod	high	none	none	low
Toxicity	high	low	mod	low	low	low	var	mod	low
Biodegradable	?	no	yes	yes	yes	yes	no#	no	yes

KEYS

mod = moderate

var = variable with formulation

? = unknown or conflicting data published

NA = not applicable

alk = alkaline

∗ Virosan™ brand is effective against pseudo-monads; other chlorhexidines are **not** effective against pseudomonads.

Wavicide™ brand name product is biodegradable.

Other disinfectant notes

- Phenols and aldehydes perform better at warmer temperatures

- Iodophores are only stable as long as dark color is maintained and may stain.

- QAC destroys chlamydia but is usually expensive.

- Alcohols evaporate rapidly and may require reapplication.

- Chlorines break down in light and solutions must be fresh. Chlorines are usually inexpensive.

Chapter 3 – BASIC REQUIREMENTS FOR HOUSING WILD ANIMALS IN REHABILITATION

3.1 Overview

Wildlife rehabilitators should be able to provide enclosures or cages of appropriate size made from appropriate materials that contain appropriate furnishings for all ages of all species that they commonly treat. The cage sizes recommended in this document are minimal, and the suggested materials work well for many rehabilitators. Alternative techniques for housing and pre-release conditioning are encouraged, but must meet basic natural history, comfort, and hygiene requirements. Assigning cage size strictly by species is not always realistic; variations in an individual's size due to race or age, and variations in an individual's behavior due to age and season, will affect appropriate cage size. Dimensions can be modified to accommodate special needs of the facility or the individual animal and new advancements in the field.

Minimum standards for enclosures are based on common sense. All enclosures should be structurally sound, constructed of materials appropriate for species housed, maintained in good repair, and designed to protect the animal from injury, abuse, or harassment while containing the animal and restricting the entrance of other animals. Enclosures should provide sufficient shelter from overheating, excessive rain, snow, or cold temperatures. Each animal should be able to turn about freely, and lie or sit comfortably, unless medically restrained. The construction material should be of sufficient strength, and be of a nonporous, waterproof finish (when reasonable) to facilitate cleaning and disinfection.

The facility should have reliable and adequate potable water and electricity available year round. Food and bedding should be stored in an appropriate manner that protects it from spoilage, infestation and contamination. Waste should be properly disposed of in accordance with all regulations, in a manner that minimizes vermin infestation, odors, and disease hazards. The facility should provide fresh air in a manner that avoids drafts, odors, and water condensation, and provides auxiliary ventilation when ambient temperature exceeds 85°F. Lighting should be adequate to allow for inspection and cleaning, while not stressing animals. Full spectrum lights may be necessary. The facility should be sufficiently drained to protect against sewage back up in traps and to rapidly eliminate water accumulation.

An effort should be made by the rehabilitator to obtain as much information as possible on each species admitted through reference and natural history literature and contact with other rehabilitators familiar with the species. Through an understanding of each species' behavior and natural history, proper choices can be made to provide suitable cage habitats.

All rehabilitators should be prepared to provide _**temporary**_ housing for any species they are likely to encounter—including those species rarely encountered, and/or for which they are not currently licensed to treat. These animals should be transferred within 24 hours to another rehabilitator or facility that is both properly licensed and equipped for their care.

Many indoor and outdoor cages can be constructed for multispecies use. These cages can be quickly modified to accommodate different species through substituting different perches or other furnishings. Thus, a separate cage is not needed for each species the rehabilitator intends to treat, but cages should be able to be adequately disinfected and adapted to meet the minimum standards required for the species.

Many young animals (e.g., fledgling crows or infant raccoons) should be group-housed with conspecifics to avoid imprinting on and/or socialization to humans. When foster parents are available, young birds (when possible) should be transferred to facilities having those foster parents. Efforts should also be made to network with other rehabilitators to place individual (single) young animals with others of its own species.

When birds are developed sufficiently to perch or mammals to ambulate, cages meeting adult requirements are necessary. These adolescents may be more "behaviorally comfortable" being group-housed with conspecifics. Group-housing is not always feasible or the best option for adults. The natural history and seasonal behavior of the species are factors to consider before housing adult animals together.

Housing design must provide for the safety of both humans and animals. In addition to the above, some important considerations include:

- Avoid areas where animals can become tangled or trapped

- Avoid sharp edges or points (inside and outside cages)

- Cages should be checked regularly for protruding objects which should be removed prior to placing animals in the cages (e.g., nails or screws backing out, bent wire)

- Allow for "running" distance for both human and animal, including hiding boxes

- Ensure proper footing by using flooring with good drainage (French drains can help to reduce standing water and soggy ground in areas under open-topped enclosures)

- Avoid ledges that can be used as unintended perches or can accumulate feces

- Secure all cages with appropriate locks

- Use food trapdoors if possible to minimize interaction

3.2 Cage Size Criteria Based on Medical Status

Appropriate cage space is conditional to the species, the behavior of the individual, the nature of the injury, and the specifics of treatment and recovery. Recommended cage dimensions are based on approximations of space requirements during three recovery periods, each defined by the activity level required of the patient(s). These levels are restricted activity/mobility, limited activity/mobility, and unlimited activity/mobility. Individual animals must each be evaluated regularly as their housing needs may change. Not every animal will require each level of caging--many may progress from restricted activity/mobility caging directly into unlimited activity/mobility caging, and those requiring only temporary care may be able to be released directly from restricted activity/mobility caging, provided the rehabilitator is able to adequately assess the animals' ability to ambulate as required by that species.

The following subsections describe the three activity levels and the caging best suited to them. Housing/caging should allow recovering animals the prescribed amount of self-imposed activity or supervised/forced activity during rehabilitation. Prescribed activity can be linked with cage size based on species and stage of recovery. Indoor caging is replaced by outdoor caging as the animal progresses through the rehabilitation process. Animals requiring large expanses of water (for example, grebes, loons, pelagic birds, and many marine mammals) present some challenges to wildlife rehabilitators and this set of activity descriptions; these descriptions may not apply directly to such species.

3.2.1 Restricted Activity/Mobility

Restricted activity/mobility means to hold an animal within a space small enough to restrict almost all movement, but to provide enough room for the animal to maintain a normal alert/upright posture and to stretch its body, limbs and tail, but not enough to leap, fly, or run. The enclosure should be small enough to facilitate easy capture, thereby minimizing capture stress and the possibility of injury during repeated periods of capture and treatment. Young mammals and birds confined to their nest prior to weaning and fledging are included in this category.

Conditions requiring restricted activity include rehydration, hypothermia, or injured or bandaged limb. Any animal with severely debilitating conditions such as shock, toxicity, neurological impairment, or other conditions that require close supervision and management should be considered as restricted activity patients.

Restricted activity areas are provided by incubators, veterinary cages, kennel carriers, and other small enclosures. Perches close to the cage floor (relative to the size of the bird) and/or walk-ups to perches should be provided depending on equilibrium and/or injury. Hiding areas such as boxes or towels must be provided for those species with more reclusive behavior such as raccoons, wrens, and rat snakes. Limited access to tubs or small pools might be provided to semiaquatic or pelagic species when the injury permits. Restricted activity is maintained primarily indoors in northern temperate areas.

3.2.2 Limited Activity/Mobility

Physical therapy and/or acclimatization comprise the next phase of the rehabilitation process once the anatomical and/or physiological problem has been corrected. Movement is now encouraged as part of the healing process. This physical therapy may be voluntary and/or provided by care-givers.

Limited activity/mobility is when restriction of the animal's movement is no longer necessary due to ongoing treatment, but periodic capture and medical treatment may still be necessary. These enclosures are also used for fledged birds and weaned mammals. Outdoor caging should provide the opportunity for short flights or walks/runs. Perches and walk-ups to perches (birds) or hiding areas and nest boxes (all animals) are appropriate furnishings. Semiaquatic and pelagic species should have access to tubs or pools of water for exercise. Creance flying may be appropriate physical therapy during this phase.

3.2.3 Unlimited Activity/Mobility

Unlimited activity/mobility uses large and complex outdoor caging. These enclosures provide physical and psychological conditioning or reconditioning through extended flights for birds and walks, runs and/or climbs for mammals. This housing should allow animals to improve their strength, develop stamina and coordination, restore muscle tone, and acclimate to ambient weather conditions. Physical therapy should be primarily voluntary although some may be forced by care-givers. Unlimited activity caging should be used to condition fledged birds and weaned mammals for release. At least two perches of differing size, with at least one under cover from extreme weather, should be provided for birds. Hiding areas and nest boxes should be provided for all animals. Large pools of water should be provided for aquatic species. Creance flying may be appropriate physical therapy during this phase as well. Please see notes on raptor housing for more specific details on how creance conditioning relates to cage size.

3.3 Natural History/Behavior

The natural history and behavior of any species must be considered in the enclosure design process. Not only does the enclosure provide for security and animal safety, it provides habitat in which the animal can learn or relearn behaviors specific to that species. Caging should provide animals undergoing rehabilitation the opportunities necessary for complete recovery from injuries and/or for learning and practicing vital behaviors and honing skills such as foraging or hunting.

Cage design and furniture should provide enrichment to address and encourage species-specific patterns of foraging, play, rest or sleep, hiding or predator avoidance, and social responses to conspecifics or cage mates. For example, many species such as crows and raccoons respond well to toys, hides, pools, climbs, and other species-appropriate enhancements. Other species, such as mourning doves and opossums seem to benefit less from such curiosity enhancements; however, even these species have been observed using these items over time. Suggestions for appropriate habitat furnishing can be found in the specific housing sections which follow, and in the reference material in Appendix C.

Animals should be fed palatable, nutritionally balanced food in a form and presentation appropriate to their natural behavior and their medical condition. Diets are highly specialized and specific dietary needs may vary from one individual to another; for this reason, a wildlife veterinarian or veterinary nutritionist should be consulted before formulating any new diets or adding vitamins or other supplements to existing diets. Some species may show strong preference for a specific food item, so efforts should be made to provide a varied diet and regularly monitor food intake and changes in body weight.

3.4 General Indoor Caging/Housing

Minimizing stress experienced by animals in rehabilitation is a key factor in the design of indoor enclosures. All indoor caging should be located in an area that provides quiet and minimal visual stimuli. Specific suggestions to minimize stressors are to cover cage doors, provide visual barriers, position cage fronts away from human activity, remove radios, and place the enclosures far from high traffic areas. When possible, natural daylight should be provided. Full-spectrum (UVB, UVA, visible light, and infrared) lighting should be used when natural lighting is not feasible. Some products are advertised as "full-spectrum" while only providing the full <u>visible</u> spectrum. The need for full-spectrum light can vary by species;

for example, snakes do not require UVB light. Any artificial light source should be timed to mimic current seasonal daylight cycles.

3.5 General Outdoor Caging/Housing

Animals undergoing rehabilitation are generally housed in outdoor enclosures prior to release. Enclosure design varies widely depending on materials used, climatic conditions, species housed, zoning regulations, building permits, and many other considerations. Large, outdoor caging provides opportunities for exercise, behavioral rehabilitation, and acclimatization to weather conditions, while smaller outdoor caging may be used for short periods prior to this release conditioning.

The philosophy dictating cage size presupposes normal recovery times for the patient. None of the restricted or limited activity sizes is recommended for extended or permanent care. Housing for animals kept permanently (e.g., for educational, exhibit or captive-breeding purposes) is not addressed in this document, but can be found elsewhere (Appendix C).

Special consideration must be made in the design of outdoor enclosures to provide adequate shelter, safety, and proper habitat for animals in rehabilitation. Enclosures should be made secure against local predators, including adequate perimeter control; for example, a cement floor and foundation or ½-inch galvanized hardware cloth buried under the cage floor and extending two feet up the walls may be considered adequate protective design. All outdoor cages should be equipped with a double-door entry system: if two physical doors cannot be constructed into a cage, a second barrier of netting, heavy plastic sheeting, or other material should be installed to prevent animal escapes. Enclosures and their contents should duplicate natural conditions wherever practical. Cage design should provide for ease of cleaning, proper ventilation, adequate light, and temperature control. A nearby source of running water will greatly facilitate cleaning of outdoor cages. Proper substrates and furnishings appropriate for each species should also be provided in each cage. Bedding substrates should be placed in areas where they will remain dry. Fresh water for drinking and/or bathing must be available in each enclosure.

Each outdoor enclosure should possess an area that provides necessary protection from the elements, yet still enables the animal to be conditioned for survival in the wild. All cages should have a roofed portion or contain a nest box or other means of protection from inclement weather, while also providing opportunities for exposure to sunlight. Feeding areas (and the food within) should be protected from the elements. Adequate air flow is important, especially in warmer climates, while making certain that protection from the wind and weather is provided on the side of enclosures receiving the prevailing weather. In northern climates, roofs and doors should be constructed to withstand the weight and depth of snowfall, and solid roof sections in all climes should be angled to allow for proper drainage, lest water collect and rot the roofing material or provide mosquito breeding habitat.

Outdoor enclosures ideally protect the animal without habituating it to human activity. To avoid habituation to humans or even taming, cages should be surrounded by a fence or somehow placed out of view of the general public. As in the design of indoor enclosures, minimal human contact, both visual and auditory, is preferable. Domestic animals and other potential predators should be prevented from contacting animals in rehabilitation, as predator avoidance is an important factor in survival of rehabilitated animals. Consideration of these variables when designing outdoor enclosures is vital for proper rehabilitation of wildlife.

Outdoor caging alone may not be adequate for full conditioning of certain species and/or certain injuries; for example, the flight conditioning requirement for successful release of a peregrine falcon recovering from a shoulder fracture may exceed that provided by any caging. The large cages or deep pools necessary for proper conditioning of some species are not available to all wildlife rehabilitators. In many instances, cooperation with other rehabilitators or wildlife professionals may ultimately be the most successful strategy an individual rehabilitator can choose. Working with licensed falconers or experienced rehabilitators to provide creancing or other pre-release training, or transferring patients to other rehabilitators with more appropriate caging, are suitable substitutes for the conditioning cages (unlimited activity) recommended in Table 5. The successful release and continued survival of rehabilitated animals is the goal of rehabilitators; networking to share information, skills and equipment is vital to the success of rehabilitation.

Chapter 4 – AVIAN HOUSING REQUIREMENTS

4.1 Overview

4.1.1 General Avian Housing Considerations

Enclosure dimensions are based on materials as well as species requirements. Exterior plywood is available in economical and easy-to-use 4-foot by 8-foot sheets and some caging dimensions have been calculated using numbers that are based on this material size. Maximum volume is achieved with cubic cages, and this fact is considered when determining cage dimensions. Enclosure design varies widely depending on materials used, climatic conditions, species housed, zoning regulations, building permits, and many other considerations. While considerable thought and experience was employed to structure the cage sizes listed in Tables 3-5, it is beyond the scope of this document to list all possibilities in terms of material, design, or size.

Cage sizes specify minimums and are determined for the species at different stages of rehabilitation. Intelligent substitution of height and ground area requirements is encouraged; for example, while pheasants and egrets are the same size, one requires ground space while the other needs height. Substitutions resulting in larger sized or differently shaped cages are encouraged.

Multiple occupancy by **compatible** species of similar ages is not only acceptable but beneficial, particularly in conditioning (unlimited activity/mobility) caging for fledgling birds. Individuals of certain other species (e.g., herons, titmice, woodpeckers, etc.) may be extremely aggressive and may require individual housing.

4.1.2 Construction Materials

Many different types of construction materials for avian enclosures are used in rehabilitation. Selection of appropriate material is important for the proper construction of adequate enclosures. In general, aviaries should have a double-door entry system (not always necessary for birds less apt to fly in confined areas, such as waterfowl and seabirds). Solid walls for aviaries can be constructed of wood, fiberglass, or an equivalent. Restricted Activity-sized cages for many birds including shorebirds, woodcocks, woodpeckers, and kingfishers, among others, can be made simply by placing a top on an empty stock tank. The smooth but rugged sides of the tank prevent feather damage, are easy to clean, and prevent escape. These tanks can be used inside an outdoor cage to begin acclimatization, but holes should be drilled in the bottom to allow for drainage in the event of rain. Hardware cloth, chicken wire, and chain-link fencing are not recommended if the birds can come into direct contact with them; these may be used if appropriate netting or screening is used on the interior surface. If vertical wood lath, fiberglass screening, or netting prevent direct contact, then wire can add extra security, may be used as the external material for most cages, and is recommended to prevent predators from reaching or entering between slats or through screening or netting.

4.1.3 Flooring Considerations

Flooring for aviaries varies with types of birds. Substrates, such as sand or pea gravel, should be changed as often as necessary depending on use and moisture content, and bi-annually at a minimum. Natural flooring is acceptable in very large enclosures. This natural flooring must be turned over and disinfected on a regular basis, depending on the number and size of birds housed in the enclosure. Irregular surfaces in outdoor aviaries may actually be beneficial as it provides natural exercising of the legs and feet; however, trip hazards and sharp surfaces should be avoided.

Flooring substrates for small cages include tight-woven towels (thick or loose weave may catch toenails), paper towels, fleece, raised netting over newspaper, newspaper alone, clean soil, or dried pine needles. [Note: Dried pine needles are not appropriate for ground-foraging birds such as doves, as crop rupture has been noted when these birds ingest the pine needles; newspaper alone is not suitable for young, growing birds or birds with leg injuries that have difficulty standing on smooth surfaces.] The selection of substrate is dependent on the species being housed.

4.1.4 General Avian Furnishings

Many types of cage furnishings are appropriate for birds undergoing rehabilitation. Bath pans or pools should be provided for all birds whose medical condition does not prohibit them from getting wet (e.g., bath pans are usually contraindicated for birds with wing wraps or foot bandages or for birds with neurologic deficits). When perching is required in outdoor caging (see Tables 3-5), each cage should have a minimum of two perches for birds capable of perching. Waterfowl and seabirds, and some other species such as nightjars, will have different "perch" requirements. Birds that are in limited or restricted activity cages may not be capable of perching; however, some mechanism should be provided to allow the bird to at least stand with its tail off the ground, and/or the bird should be fitted with a tail guard to protect tail feathers from breaking or becoming soiled.

Perches and all surface substrates (both those on floors and perches) should be customized to the appropriate size and material for the species using them. Appropriate size and substrate will vary with the natural history of the species (e.g., limb-perchers vs. ledge perchers) and should be designed with the goal of minimizing foot damage. Using a variety of substrates such as ¼-inch-pile Astroturf™, Daisy Mat™, Nomad™, hemp, or coco-mat to cover the perches helps tremendously to achieve this goal. Perches should be of a minimum height to allow the tail feathers to be off the floor; the maximum height should be determined based on the bird's injury and natural history. Perches should be placed and constructed in such a manner to prevent the bird from becoming lodged or getting a wing caught if it is startled and jumps or falls off the perch. Perches also should be placed an adequate distance from bare slatted walls to prevent raccoons or other predators from reaching a bird asleep on the perch; alternatively, predator wire can be added to the outside of the wood slatted section adjacent to where the perch meets the slatted wall. At least one perch should be located in a covered, protected area (preferably the highest perch, as that is the one most likely to be selected as a roost perch), and at least one perch should be located so that the bird can be exposed to direct sunlight and the elements. Outdoor caging for all avian species should provide appropriate shelter, either via solid roof coverings or hide boxes/areas, and at least some portion of the wall should be solid for the same purpose. Nest boxes and shelters provide a natural space that reduces stress and enhances security. Appropriate sized substitute nests and incubators of the proper temperature and humidity should be provided for nestling birds (Gage & Duerr 2007 and other resources for species specific suggestions).

4.2 Housing for Songbirds

4.2.1 General Songbird Housing Considerations

The songbird (passerine or perching) group of birds includes a large number of individual species with wide ranges in size, behavior, habitat, foraging techniques, food items, and subsequent rehabilitation requirements. These requirements must be understood and addressed to ensure successful rehabilitation and eventual release of healthy, well-adapted individuals that are prepared for survival in the wild.

Understanding the natural history of any species in rehabilitation is necessary when considering caging arrangements. Songbirds have many natural predators such as hawks, owls, other birds, snakes, and small mammals, as well as domestic animals associated with man (cats and dogs). Care should be taken to reduce exposure of these birds to potential predators, thereby reducing stress and/or potential injury. While some species may be housed together within this group, especially when young, some species such as jays and crows are predators of other species. Songbirds that are seed-eaters or omnivores have characteristic heavy beaks with the capacity to harm birds with much smaller insectivorous beaks. Certain other species can be aggressive towards other birds, including their own species.

The requirements for pre-release conditioning (unlimited activity) caging vary greatly among songbird species. White-breasted nuthatches, bushtits, and titmice generally fly straight from their nests, requiring very little pre-fledge training. Caging for these birds need not be as high or large as other songbirds for this reason; shorter caging may be elevated on platforms to make access easier (so that a person can reach into the cage at waist-height rather than having to stoop to enter a short cage). Elevating smaller cages also places these songbirds in a physically higher and thus more natural and comfortable location. Elevated cages should be constructed within a larger cage or other enclosed area to facilitate recapture if a bird escapes. Larger birds, such as robins, mockingbirds, and jays, leave the nest early and spend a lot of time on the ground while developing flight feathers. During this time, the fledglings follow the adults and learn appropriate survival behaviors. Larger songbirds require exercise and practice to fly well so a larger aviary is recommended to house these species.

Songbird cages that are located in suitable habitats can be equipped with release hatches on one side. The hatch can be lowered/opened at the appropriate time of day to allow for a 'soft release' in which the birds can leave the cage at their own will; this technique reduces stress and potential injury by eliminating the need to capture the birds for release. Songbirds that need to be released at an alternative location can be captured from the outdoor cage at night when they are generally calmer and less stressed, housed indoors overnight, and released the following morning.

4.2.2 Construction Materials

External wire on outdoor caging for songbirds should be ½" x ½" galvanized hardware cloth (or 1/2" x 1" welded rat wire) to prevent access by predators. The use of chicken wire or chain-link is not recommended, as the large openings allow predator entry or accidental escape of cage inhabitants if the interior lining becomes torn or loosened. Interior walls should be lined with screening or a very fine-meshed netting, such as shade-cloth. Mesh size is important, as large mesh may allow songbirds to catch toenails or even toes in the netting. Fiberglass screening is acceptable for most songbirds, but will not withstand the pecking behavior of titmice, jays, woodpeckers, and some other species. Wire screening has been used successfully without causing damage to feathers.

Selection of surface material depends on the natural history of the species being housed. No wood surfaces should be exposed in cages for Piciformes, as they will destroy these surfaces. Interior surfaces may be lined with metal or plastic siding, and may prevent the birds from climbing (thereby preventing feather damage). PVC pipe, reinforced with rebar inside, makes effective, indestructible cage framing and perches for larger woodpeckers.

Floors of both indoor and outdoor cages should be composed of or covered with appropriate substances to prevent slipping (splay leg) and/or bumblefoot. Suitable substrates to improve footing include, but are not limited to, newspaper, towels, paper toweling, foamy plastic shelf liner, sand, Astroturf™, and parasite-free dried pine needles. [Note: Dried pine needles are not appropriate for ground-foraging birds such as doves, as crop rupture has been noted when these birds ingest the pine needles.]

4.2.3 Furnishings

Understanding the natural history of the species being rehabilitated, and then adapting the aviary accordingly for that species, can give the bird(s) a great advantage when released. Woodpeckers do well when raised with hollow logs for a nest; bushtits, on the other hand, are raised very well when they have a hanging sock for a nest and food is provided for them to find on tree branches and leaves throughout their aviary. Cavity dwellers/nesters should be provided with some sort of hide box or cavity-type container. Fleece and tight-woven towels (like surgical towels) can be draped over cage walls to provide vertical clinging surfaces for swifts, nuthatches, woodpeckers, etc. of all ages. Aviaries that are furnished with natural plantings help reduce stress and provide the birds with natural shading, perching, hiding, and foraging opportunities. Earthtones and other natural pastel colors (for interior walls, bedding, and other furnishings) may provide some camouflage and help to reduce stress.

Table 3: Minimum Housing Guidelines for Songbirds & Misc. Avian Orders

Note: This table is not intended to be used independently; it should be used only in conjunction with the information in Chapter 4, Sections 4.1 and 4.2

Order		Length of Bird	Restricted Activity (W × L × H)	Limited Activity (W × L × H)	Unlimited Activity (W × L × H)	Max #	Codes
Columbiformes (Pigeons, Doves)	>	9 in / 23 cm	12 × 12 × 12 in / 30 × 30 × 30 cm	12 × 12 × 12 in / 30 × 30 × 30 cm	16 × 8 × 8 ft / 4.9 × 2.4 × 2.4 m	8 pigeons / 12 doves	P, Pi, Q
Cuculiformes (Cuckoos)	<	12 in / 30 cm	18 × 18 × 18 in / 46 × 46 × 46 cm	24 × 24 × 24 in / 61 × 61 × 61 cm	8 × 8 × 8 ft / 2.4 × 2.4 × 2.4 m	4 – 6	P, Q
	>	12 in / 30 cm	24 × 24 × 24 in / 61 × 61 × 61 cm	36 × 36 × 36 in / 91 × 91 × 91 cm	16 × 8 × 8 ft / 4.9 × 2.4 × 2.4 m		
Caprimulgiformes (Nighthawks, Goatsuckers)	~	9 in / 23 cm	12 × 12 × 12 in / 30 × 30 × 30 cm	12 × 24 × 12 in / 30 × 61 × 30 cm	8 × 16 × 8 ft / 2.4 × 4.9 × 2.4 m	6	C, P
Apodiformes							
Apodidae (Swifts)	<	9 in / 23 cm	12 × 12 × 12 in / 30 × 30 × 30 cm	12 × 12 × 12 in / 30 × 30 × 30 cm	8 × 8 × 8 ft / 2.4 × 2.4 × 2.4 m	15 – 20	B, Ch
Trochilidae (Hummingbirds)	<	5 in / 13 cm	7 × 11 × 5 in / 18 × 28 × 13 cm	12 × 17 × 7 in / 30 × 43 × 18 cm	2 × 4 × 6 ft / 0.6 × 1.2 × 1.8 m	4	P, Z
Coraciiformes (Kingfishers)	<	9 in / 23 cm	12 × 12 × 12 in / 30 × 30 × 30 cm	18 × 18 × 18 in / 46 × 46 × 46 cm	8 × 16 × 8 ft / 2.4 × 4.9 × 2.4 m	4	C, F, Pi, Q, S
Piciformes (Woodpeckers)	<	9 in / 23 cm	12 × 12 × 12 in / 30 × 30 × 30 cm	18 × 18 × 18 in / 46 × 46 × 46 cm	4 × 8 × 8 ft / 1.2 × 2.4 × 2.4 m	2 – 4	C, D, H, W
	>	9 in / 23 cm	18 × 18 × 18 in / 46 × 46 × 46 cm	24 × 24 × 24 in / 61 × 61 × 61 cm	8 × 16 × 8 ft / 2.4 × 4.9 × 2.4 m		
Passeriformes (Perching & Songbirds, Swallows) & **Small**	<	5 in / 13 cm	7 × 11 × 5 in / 18 × 28 × 13 cm	12 × 17 × 17 in / 30 × 43 × 43 cm	2 × 4 × 4 ft / 0.6 × 1.2 × 1.2 m	4	H, P, Z
Corvidae (Jays, Magpies, and small Crows)		5-10 in / 13-26 cm	12 × 12 × 12 in / 30 × 30 × 30 cm	18 × 18 × 18 in / 46 × 46 × 46 cm	4 × 8 × 8 ft / 1.2 × 2.4 × 2.4 m	4 - 6	H, P, Z, W
	>	17 in / 43 cm	14 × 18 × 18 in / 36 × 46 × 46 cm	24 × 18 × 24 in / 61 × 46 × 61 cm	8 × 16 × 8 ft / 2.4 × 4.9 × 2.4 m		
Corvidae (Large Crows & Ravens)	>	17 in / 43 cm	16 × 22 × 22 in / 41 × 56 × 56 cm	24 × 24 × 24 in / 61 × 61 × 61 cm	10 × 30 × 12 ft / 3.0 × 9.1 × 3.6 m	6	P
Galliformes (Quail, Pheasants)	<	20 in / 51 cm	2 × 2 × 2 ft / 0.6 × 0.6 × 0.6 m	3 × 3 × 3 ft / 0.9 × 0.9 × 0.9 m	4 × 4 × 8 ft / 1.2 × 1.2 × 2.4 m	4	H
	>	20 in / 51 cm	3 × 3 × 3 ft / 0.9 × 0.9 × 0.9 m	4 × 4 × 8 ft / 1.2 × 1.2 × 2.4 m	8 × 12 × 8 ft / 2.4 × 3.7 × 2.4 m		

Codes for Special Housing Requirements Used in Table 3, Songbirds & Misc.

B   Special vertical surfaces needed for swifts. Temporary confinement and recovery housing must be lined on all sides with a snag-free fabric or other material with enough texture for the birds to cling vertically. Two or more walls of the conditioning housing must be constructed of or covered with a roughly-textured material such as cork, rough-textured siding, or fiberglass window screening.

C   Birds such as woodpeckers and nuthatches require angled and/or vertical logs for climbing, and hollow logs for hiding/nesting. These logs also help to maintain beak and foot health, and allow the birds foraging experience as they hunt for ants, grubs, etc. Birds such as kingfishers and nighthawks require large, horizontal, elevated logs several inches wide for perching; flat rocks also may provide suitable perches.

Ch A waist-high "artificial chimney" should be located in the center of the outdoor housing as a feeding station or roost; suggestions for construction may be found in Kyle, P. and G. Kyle, 1995.

D   Birds with this designation require old logs, etc., as drumming materials.

F   Special substrate needed. These species are susceptible to foot problems. Depending on the species, padded flooring, towels, linens/sheeting, carpets, natural low-dust kitty litter (no additives), or sand may be used.

H   Hides; provide natural vegetative material or human-devised areas for cover. (All birds will benefit from an area of cover.)

P   Requires two or more perches of varied diameter; materials may be natural branches, hemp or sisal rope from ¼" to ¾" diameter, dowel rods covered with self-adhering wrap (such as Vetrap™ 3M, St. Paul, MN), or other suitable substances (such as rubber drawer-liners). Varied substrates, diameters, and locations allow the bird choices and minimize captivity-related foot problems.

Pi Piling or shelves required for perching; these may be covered with Astroturf™ or other suitable material to provide good footing and prevent bumblefoot lesions.

Q   Quiet and extreme privacy required (very prone to stress).

S   Bathing area required.

W   Large pan with soil, leaves, grass and/or wood chips containing live worms, grubs, mealworms and/or insects to allow the birds to forage on their own. May not be required for all species in the orders listed - check natural history requirements.

Z   Although larger conditioning cage sizes may be preferred, great care must be taken to seal off small openings or cracks that can act as traps.

(WxLxH) = Listed in order: Width x Length x Height

in = inches   ft = feet   cm = centimeters   m = meters

~ = approximately   < = less than   > = greater than

Max # = Maximum recommended number of conspecifics housed in "Unlimited Activity" enclosure; actual number will vary with season, age, and temperament of individual birds.

4.3 Housing for Waterbirds

4.3.1 General Waterbird Housing Considerations

Waterbirds, as the name implies, are those birds that spend much of their time in, on, or around the water. Consequently, feathers are a critical component to their survival.

Many species of waterbirds, including alcids, loons, grebes, fulmars, petrels, shearwaters, and sea ducks, spend nearly their entire life in water and cannot live without feathers that keep them waterproof. These birds have many anatomical adaptations to a life spent primarily on the water. The delicate nature of the skin on the plantar surfaces of their feet and the caudal position of their legs on the body predispose many species to pressure lesions in a captive environment out of water. Proper housing is a key component to preventing feather contamination (which causes loss of waterproofing), pressure lesions, and other secondary complications that can delay or even prevent successful rehabilitation.

Caging for birds unable to be housed in water

Indoor caging for some aquatic birds should have a net-bottom in which the floor of the cage is made of netting material and sides are made of a non rigid material. The netting material serves two purposes: 1) providing a forgiving surface on which a bird's keel can rest with decreased pressure and 2) allowing fecal material to pass away from the bird, minimizing feather contamination. In addition to the net bottom caging, preventative wraps like keel protectors, foot booties, and hock wraps should be applied to appropriate species being housed out of water.

- Net bottom pens should be used when these species are temporarily housed out of water to help mitigate pressure lesions and prevent fecal contamination of their feathers. The net bottoms provide increased ventilation and allow feces to fall to the floor instead of accumulating on birds feathers, thereby preventing feather rot & contamination. The top should be covered with a visual barrier like a sheet or shade cloth.
- Soft sided caging should be used for flighty species prone to carpal wounds (i.e., waterfowl, sea ducks) and for long-boned birds (i.e., herons and egrets) housed in restricted/limited caging indoors.

Reducing time spent out of water

Progressing waterbirds quickly through the rehabilitation process to a state that allows them to be housed in an aqueous enclosure is the ultimate preventative treatment to avoid these secondary complications.

All of these birds require some sort of pool in their outdoor (unlimited activity) caging. The size of the pool varies greatly from species to species and with the individual injury. The natural feeding, drinking, and bathing behavior of each species should be considered in the design of the pool, including depth of the water for swimming, bathing, and drinking. For example, sandhill cranes dip and scoop to drink water, so this species requires a water bowl with a minimum diameter of 12" and a minimum depth of 5".

- All pools should have an overflow to prevent contamination from diet & feces, and a visual barrier. Appropriate perching or haul out should be offered.

- Aviaries with a pool should have ramps in and out of the water, substrate and perches appropriate for the species, a visual barrier, and an overflow.
- Low perches or perches placed on the ground (for perching birds) can be offered to individuals with injuries affecting normal ambulation.

The cage sizes recommended in this manual are minimal. Every bird would benefit from as large a flight area as possible and the rehabilitator is encouraged to construct larger cages whenever reasonable. The recommendations throughout the *Minimum Standards* have been tried by experienced rehabilitators and shown to be those minimally acceptable for safe and effective rehabilitation of the species indicated. Remember that large cages intended for animals with greater space requirements can be designed to be subdivided or furnished for other species when needed.

Many of these birds are colonial foragers and nesters. Group housing for species that are colonial waterbirds may reduce stress and promote natural behavior; however, during nesting season, even these birds will have some 'personal' territorial needs. As a result, fewer birds may be able to be housed together during nesting season than in non-breeding season. Other birds are gregarious and do well in social groups, but are not as stressed if kept individually. A precise knowledge of the species' natural history will help in determining if the birds in rehabilitation are too territorial for group housing, or what the optimum number of individuals might be for any given enclosure dimensions. Maximum numbers of birds housed together is usually a factor of actual cage size, season, behavior of individual birds, and the ability to maintain cage sanitation/water quality and protect feather condition. Birds should be monitored closely when introduced to co-housing situations, and periodically thereafter.

4.3.2 Construction Materials

Construction materials for aquatic birds are similar to those required for most other avian species. All materials should be easy to clean and disinfect. Use materials that are impervious to water or that can be sealed to become impervious. Materials utilized for walls should provide visual barriers, minimize chances of injury, provide adequate ventilation, and protect against predators and domestic animals. Pool materials include galvanized metals, plastics, fiberglass, cement, and natural ponds. Any sharp or abrasive areas should be covered to prevent injury and substrates should be appropriate to prevent injuries to feet, e.g., matting, on flat surfaces such as cement, wood, or fiberglass.

Most waterbirds spend the majority of their time in or near large bodies of water and are conditioned to seeing open sky overhead; thus, the majority of the roof on an outdoor cage should be open, allowing for a clear view of the sky and providing sufficient ventilation to reduce the risk of aspergillosis. Netting works well for this application and will prevent injury from collisions if the birds fly upwards. This type of construction is psychologically beneficial to the birds, and it encourages them to exercise.

Many waterbirds spend little to virtually no time on land; when out of water for medical purposes or due to poor waterproofing, these birds should be housed on tightly-stretched, suspended netting (species noted with an 'N' in table 4; Holcomb 1988 and Tegtmeier 2005 provide more information on construction).

(continued on Page 44)

Table 4: Minimum Housing Guidelines for Waterbirds

Note: This table is not intended to be used independently; it should be used only in conjunction with the information in Chapter 4, Sections 4.1 and 4.3

Order	Restricted Activity (W × L × H)	Limited Activity (W × L × H)	Unlimited Activity (W × L × H)	Codes
Gaviiformes				
Loons	15 in × 30 in × 30 in 38 cm × 76 cm × 76 cm	3 ft × 3 ft × 3 ft 0.9 m × 0.9 m × 0.9 m	Pool: 8 ft diam. × 2 ft deep 2.4 m × 0.6 m	N, PT, PP, SO Col/Sol
Podicipediformes				
Small grebes (Eared, Horned & Pied-billed)	12 in × 12 in × 12 in 30 cm × 30 cm × 30 cm	18 in × 18 in × 18 in 46 cm × 46 cm × 46 cm	Pool: 6 ft diam. × 2 ft deep 1.8 m × 0.6 m	N, H, PT, PP, SO Col/Sol
Large grebes (Western, Clark's & Red-necked)	18 in × 18 in × 18 in 46 cm × 46 cm × 46 cm	2 ft × 2 ft × 2 ft 0.6 m × 0.6 m × 0.6 m	Pool: 6 ft diam. × 2 ft deep 1.8 m × 0.6 m	N, PT, PP, SO Col/Sol
Procellariiformes				
Storm-petrels	12 in × 12 in × 12 in 30 cm × 30 cm × 30 cm	18 in × 18 in × 18 in 46 cm × 46 cm × 46 cm	Pool: 45 in diam. × 8 in deep 114 cm × 20 cm	N, PT, PP, SO, AG Col/Terr
Large petrels, Fulmar & Shearwaters	18 in × 18 in × 18 in 46 cm × 46 cm × 46 cm	3 ft × 3 ft × 2 ft 0.9 m × 0.9 m × 0.6 m	Pool: 6 ft diam. × 12 in deep 1.8 m × 30 cm	N, PT, PP, SO, AG Col/Terr
Albatrosses	3 ft × 3 ft × 3 ft 0.9 m × 0.9 m × 0.9 m	4 ft × 6 ft × 4 ft 1.2 m × 1.8 m × 1.2 m	Pool: 10 ft diam. × 18 in deep 3.0 m × 46 cm	N, PT, PP, SO, AG Col/Terr
Pelecaniformes				
Pelicans (Brown)	3 ft × 3 ft × 3 ft 0.9 m × 0.9 m × 0.9 m	4 ft × 8 ft × 4 ft 1.2 m × 2.4 m × 1.2 m	Pool: 10 ft diam. × 2 ft deep 3.0 m × 0.6 m Aviary: 15 ft × 30 ft × 12 ft 4.5 m × 9.0 m × 3.6 m	PT, AP, SO Col/Terr
Pelicans (White)	4 ft × 4 ft × 4 ft 1.2 m × 1.2 m × 1.2 m	4 ft × 8 ft × 4 ft 1.2 m × 2.4 m × 1.2 m	Pool: 10 ft diam. × 2 ft deep 3.0 m × 0.6 m Aviary: 15 ft × 30 ft × 12 ft 4.5 m × 9.0 m × 3.6 m	PT, AP, SO Col/Terr
Gannets, Boobies,	3 ft × 3 ft × 3 ft 0.9 m × 0.9 m × 0.9 m	4 ft × 8 ft × 4 ft 1.2 m × 2.4 m × 1.2 m	Pool: 8 ft diam. × 2 ft deep 2.4 m × 0.6 m Aviary: 8 ft × 16 ft × 8 ft 2.4 m × 4.9 m × 2.4 m	PT, AP, SO, ST Col/Terr

Order	Bird Size	Restricted Activity (W × L × H)	Limited Activity (W × L × H)	Unlimited Activity (W × L × x × H)	Codes
Cormorants, Anhingas, & Tropicbirds		24 in × 30 in × 30 in / 60 cm × 90 cm × 90 cm	4 ft × 6 ft × 4 ft / 1.2 m × 1.8 m × 1.2 m	Pool: 8 ft × 20 ft × 2 × 10 ft / 2.4 m × 6.0 m × 0.6 m × 3.0 m Aviary: 8 ft / 2.4 m	PT, AP, SO, ST, Col/Terr
Frigatebirds		3 ft × 6 ft × 3 ft / 0.9 m × 1.8 m × 0.9 m	4 ft × 6 ft × 8 ft / 1.2 m × 1.8 m × 2.4 m	Pool: None required Aviary: 12 ft × 30 ft × 12 ft / 3.6 m × 9.0 m × 3.6 m	ST, Sol
Ciconiiformes					
Bitterns, Herons & Egrets*	< 20 in / 51 cm	18 in × 18 in × 24 in / 46 cm × 46 cm × 60 cm	2 ft × 2 ft × 4 ft / 0.6 m × 0.6 m × 1.2 m	Wading Pool: 2-3 ft / .6-.9 m × diam. × 6-10 in / 15-25 cm deep	AW, AG
				Aviary: 4 ft × 12 ft × 8 ft / 1.2 m × 3.7 m × 2.4 m	Terr
Bitterns, Herons, Egrets, Storks, Ibis & Spoonbill*	> 20 in / 51 cm	3 ft × 3 ft × 3 ft / 0.9 m × 0.9 m × 0.9 m	4 ft × 8 ft × 6 ft / 1.2 m × 2.4 m × 1.8 m	Wading Pool: 5-6 ft / 1.5-2 m × diam. × 6-10 in / 15-25 cm deep	AW
				Aviary: 10 ft × 25 ft × 10 ft / 3.0 m × 7.6 m × 3.0 m	Terr
Anseriformes					
Swans		4 ft × 4 ft × 4 ft / 1.2 m × 1.2 m × 1.2 m	4 ft × 8 ft × 4 ft / 1.2 m × 2.4 m × 1.2 m	Wading Pool: 8 ft / 2.4 m × diam. × 2 / 0.6 × 2 ft / 0.6 m deep	PT, AP
				Aviary: 12 ft × 20 ft × 8 ft / 3.7 m × 6.1 m × 2.4 m	Gre but Terr
Geese		3 ft × 3 ft × 3 ft / 0.9 m × 0.9 m × 0.9 m	4 ft × 6 ft × 4 ft / 1.2 m × 1.8 m × 1.2 m	Wading Pool: 6 ft / 1.8 m × diam. × 2 / 0.6 × 2 ft / 0.6 m deep	PT, AP
				Aviary: 10 ft × 18 ft × 8 ft / 3.0 m × 5.5 m × 2.4 m	Gre but Terr
**Marsh Ducks & Whistling Ducks (dabblers)		18 in × 18 in × 12 in / 46 cm × 46 cm × 30 cm	2 ft × 2 ft × 2 ft / 0.6 m × 0.6 m × 0.6 m	Wading Pool: 45 in / 114 cm × diam. × 8 / 20 × 8 in / 20 cm deep	ON, PT, AP
				Aviary: 6 ft × 10 ft × 8 ft / 1.8 m × 3.0 m × 2.4 m	Gre but Terr
Bay Ducks^, Sea Ducks^^ & Mergansers (divers)		18 in × 18 in × 12 in / 46 cm × 46 cm × 30 cm	2 ft × 2 ft × 2 ft / 0.6 m × 0.6 m × 0.6 m	Pool: 6 ft / 1.8 m × diam. × 2 / 0.6 × 2 ft / 0.6 m deep	N, PT, PP, SO
					Gre but Terr

Order	Bird Size	Restricted Activity (W × L × H)	Limited Activity (W × L × H)	Unlimited Activity	Codes
Gruiformes					
Cranes		3 ft × 3 ft × 4 ft (0.9 m × 0.9 m × 1.2 m)	4 ft × 8 ft × 8 ft (1.2 m × 2.4 m × 2.4 m)	Aviary: 10 ft × 10 ft (3.0 m × 3 m); Wading Pool: 4 ft × 25 ft diam. × 4-10 in deep (1.2 m × 7.6 m × 10-25 cm)	AW
Rails*	< 10 in (25 cm)	12 in × 12 in × 12 in (30 cm × 30 cm × 30 cm)	18 in × 18 in × 18 in (46 cm × 46 cm × 46 cm)	Wading Pool: 3 ft × 6 ft diam. × 3-5 in deep (0.9 m × 1.8 m × 8-13 cm); Aviary: 4 ft × 6 ft × 6 ft (1.2 m × 1.8 m × 1.8 m)	Gre but Terr; H, AW, FP; Sol
Gruiformes (continued) Rails, Gallinules & Coots*	> 10 in (25 cm)	18 in × 18 in × 18 in (46 cm × 46 cm × 46 cm)	2 ft × 2 ft × 2 ft (0.6 m × 0.6 m × 0.6 m)	Wading Pool: 45 in diam. × 8 in deep (114 cm × 20 cm); Aviary: 4 ft × 8 ft × 8 ft (1.2 m × 2.4 m × 2.4 m)	H, AW, FP; Rails = Sol / Gal & Coot = Gre
Charadriiformes					
Phalaropes		12 in × 12 in × 12 in (30 cm × 30 cm × 30 cm)	18 in × 18 in × 18 in (46 cm × 46 cm × 46 cm)	Wading Pool: 45 in diam. × 6-8 in deep (114 cm × 15-20 cm); Aviary: With SMALL land area (pool ledge)	FP, PT, PP, SO; Gre but Terr
Sandpipers, Plovers & Shorebirds* (excluding Phalaropes)	< 10 in (25 cm)	12 in × 12 in × 12 in (30 cm × 30 cm × 30 cm)	18 in × 18 in × 18 in (46 cm × 46 cm × 46 cm)	Wading Pool: 3 ft × 3 ft diam. × 1-3 in deep (0.9 m × 0.9 m × 3-8 cm); Aviary: 4 ft × 6 ft × 6 ft (1.2 m × 1.8 m × 1.8 m)	AW, FP; Gre but Terr
Sandpipers, Shorebirds & Avocets*	> 10 in (25 cm)	12 in × 18 in × 18 in (30 cm × 46 cm × 46 cm)	2 ft × 2 ft × 2 ft (0.6 m × 0.6 m × 0.6 m)	Wading Pool: 3 ft × 3 ft diam. × 3-5 in deep (0.9 m × 0.9 m × 8-13 cm); Aviary: 4 ft × 8 ft × 8 ft (1.2 m × 2.4 m × 2.4 m)	AW, FP; Gre but Terr
Gulls*	< 14 in (36 cm)	12 in × 15 in × 18 in (30 cm × 38 cm × 46 cm)	18 in × 18 in × 18 in (46 cm × 46 cm × 46 cm)	Wading Pool: 45 in × 45 in diam. × 10 in deep (114 cm × 114 cm × 25 cm); Aviary: 6 ft × 12 ft × 6 ft (1.8 m × 3.7 m × 1.8 m)	PT, AP, SO; Gre but Terr
Gulls*	> 14 in (36 cm)	18 in × 18 in × 18 in (46 cm × 46 cm × 46 cm)	3 ft × 3 ft × 3 ft (0.9 m × 0.9 m × 0.9 m)	Wading Pool: 45 in × 45 in diam. × 12 in deep (114 cm × 114 cm × 30 cm); Aviary: 8 ft × 16 ft × 8 ft (2.4 m × 4.9 m × 2.4 m)	ON, PT, AP, SO; Gre but Terr
Skimmers, Terns, Oystercatchers, Jaegers & Skuas		18 in × 18 in × 18 in (46 cm × 46 cm × 46 cm)	3 ft × 3 ft × 3 ft (0.9 m × 0.9 m × 0.9 m)	Wading Pool: 45 in × 45 in diam. × 2-6 in deep (114 cm × 114 cm × 5-15 cm); Aviary: 8 ft × 16 ft × 8 ft (2.4 m × 4.9 m × 2.4 m)	ON, AP, SO, FP, PT[see NOTE]; Gre but Terr
Auks (Alcids)*	< 12 in (30 cm)	12 in × 12 in × 18 in (30 cm × 30 cm × 46 cm)	18 in × 18 in × 18 in (46 cm × 46 cm × 46 cm)	Pool: 6 ft × 6 ft diam. × 2 ft deep (1.8 m × 1.8 m × 0.6 m)	N, PT, PP, SO, Col
Auks (Alcids)*	> 12 in (30 cm)	12 in × 18 in × 18 in (30 cm × 46 cm × 46 cm)	2 ft × 2 ft × 2 ft (0.6 m × 0.6 m × 0.6 m)	Pool: 6 ft × 6 ft diam. × 2 ft deep (1.8 m × 1.8 m × 0.6 m)	N, PT, PP, SO, Col

Key to Table 4: Minimum Housing Guidelines for Waterbirds

(WxLxH) = Listed in order: Width x Length x Height

diam = diameter

* This measurement represents the length of the bird from tip of beak to tip of tail with neck fully extended

** These include: black, gadwall, mallard, pintail, wigeon, wood, shoveler, teal

^These include: scoters, eiders, harlequin, oldsquaw

^^These include: canvasback, redhead, ring-necked, scaups, goldeneyes, bufflehead, ruddy

ft = feet

m = meter

in = inch

cm = centimeter

Codes for Special Housing Requirements Used in Table 4, Waterbirds

AG   Note that these birds can be extremely aggressive, even with conspecifics. Use caution and observe the birds' interactions when introduced, before housing together unattended.

AP   These birds require pre-release conditioning (unlimited activity) aviaries that contain pools to swim in and standing/perching surfaces.

AW   These birds require pre-release conditioning (unlimited activity) aviaries that contain shallow wading pools and a variety of perches, especially up high.

FP   These birds have very sensitive feet. Provide as much wading area (in addition to "swimming" pool) as possible in Limited and Unlimited Activity housing to help prevent husbandry injuries. The wading areas should have mud or sand substrates on the bottom for foraging, avoiding cement or other hard, rough surfaces that might damage feet.

H   Hides; provide natural vegetative material or human-devised areas for cover.

N   Should be housed on tightly stretched, suspended netting as a substrate whenever bird is not in water.

ON   When an individual of these species is housed inside and is emaciated (pronounced keel) or not standing, it should be housed on net bottom caging to protect feathers and keel until standing normally and of normal weight. Otherwise, when standing normally and keel is not extremely pronounced, housing substrate is solid and covered with toweling or matting.

PP   These species, during pre-release conditioning, require only pool space. Prior to release, individuals must be able to stay in pool full time, without a haul-out area for a minimum of 48 hours without compromise to their waterproofing.

PT   During recovery, bird should be allowed pool time as long and as often as medical condition allows (minimum 3 feet [90 cm] diameter). This may include cold or warm water pools as appropriate for individuals. NOTE: These species require graduated pools, with the depth proportionate to their size (e.g., shallower for small terns and skimmers); these species may drown in a kiddie pool.

SO   Surface overflow of pool required to maintain water quality (this can be achieved by constantly running a hose or by overflowing pool, filtering, and recirculating water).

ST   As soon as they are standing, these stiff-tail-feathered birds should have a stump or stump-like perch to avoid feather breakage and soiling.

Gre Social or gregarious; can usually be housed with other individuals of same species and often with like birds of other species; may be territorial to varying degrees in breeding/nesting season

Terr These birds are often social, but may be territorial in breeding/nesting season. Territory size needs may vary from a few feet to the entire cage, so check natural history and anticipate housing fewer individuals together during breeding/nesting season.

Col These birds are colonial and tend to do better when housed together with other individuals of the same species; may need to house fewer together during breeding/nesting season.

Sol These birds are solitary and generally do best when housed alone; when group-housed, they require individual hides and may defend these territories within the cage.

4.3.3 Furnishings

Some factors in successful habitat construction are species-specific:

- Frigatebirds have some unique problems worth considering when housing them for rehabilitation. Their tail and primary feathers are long and fragile, requiring tall pens and perches that will keep their tails off the floor. In addition, although frigatebirds naturally feed and drink on the wing, if they land on the water, they are unable to take off and will drown. For this reason, pools should not be used in their cages, and long flight cages are needed for sufficient exercise.

- Gannets, loons, and other diving species require deep pools and often will not even enter a shallow pool such as a kiddie pool. Rocks or short pilings for perches are required for gannets and some other divers, but should never be used for loons and grebes as these types of perches are too high and would cause keel damage if used. If waterproof, loons and grebes will remain in the water rather than perch; if not waterproof, netted floats or padded haul-out areas should be provided for these species. These netted floats should be large enough for the body size of the number of the birds present in the pool; multiple small floats (or haul-outs) or one large float may be used when birds are housed together. The cumulative float size should not cover more than 1/4 of the pool area in order to encourage birds to spend time in the water. Haul-outs used for loons, grebes, and other species that spend most of their life in water should only be used short term while the bird is regaining waterproofing. Once these birds are stable and waterproof the haul-out (float) should be removed. Prolonged use of a haul-out (float) can exacerbate an existing pressure lesion or contribute to the development of them.

- Frigatebirds, loons, gannets, and some other seabirds require considerable distance to take flight, and even more to sustain it. Caging cannot adequately provide ample flight space, so the goal with these species is to provide them with the ability to exercise their wings enough to prepare them for sustained flight.

- Cranes require tall cages to prevent head trauma as they tend to jump rapidly upwards. Some cranes bathe regularly, requiring pools up to 10" in depth. Because they are wading birds, the depth should be graduated.

- Terns and Oystercatchers will fly over and feed off of water, but they do not float or bathe in deep water. These species benefit from graduated pools, with the depth proportionate to their size (e.g., shallower for smaller terns).

- Skimmers, like frigatebirds, do not swim; they only feed and drink on the fly. These birds are at risk of drowning if given pools more than two inches deep.

- Pools set up for live-prey for herons and other long-billed wading birds should have several inches of soft substrate on the bottom (e.g., mud or sand) in order to avoid damage to the bill as it strikes the bottom.

4.4 Housing for Raptors

4.4.1 General Raptor Housing Considerations

Sizing for raptor housing is based on a combination of the size and flight styles of the bird. While the cage information states a minimum rectangular size (Table 5), it has been found that L-shaped and circular enclosures are often better to evaluate flight and banking abilities. As with other caging, the rehabilitator is encouraged to expand and enhance these minimum requirements, and create caging most suitable to their location, facility, caseload, and experience, keeping in mind the natural behavioral and physical needs of the birds.

Most individuals of the same species of raptors can be housed together; general exceptions are accipiters, falcons of the opposite sex, and human imprints. Arent (2007) provides a list of combinations of raptor species that has been housed together successfully.

If raptors of different species and sizes are kept near each other in separate enclosures, a visual barrier is recommended.

The needs of raptors present several challenges to achieve successful release. Generally, these birds are large predators that hunt on the wing and some migrate long distances. Appropriate conditioning is crucial not only for foraging, but for territory defense, migration, and other behaviors. Thus, it is strongly recommended that the cage dimensions listed be followed or increased. Certain species, such as the bird-catching peregrine falcon, may require additional conditioning. Hacking for nestlings, falconry exercise for better evaluation after injury, hunt training, and conditioning may be necessary for some species. Creance flying may be used for evaluation and conditioning. Hunt training or live prey testing should be arranged when hunting ability is questionable, except for those birds hacked out or fostered into nests. Creance flying should not take the place of hunt training. Guidelines found in *Reconditioning Raptors: A Training Manual For The Creance Technique* (Arent, L. 2000) are recommended. Guidelines for hacking young raptors can be found in *Hacking: A Method for Releasing Peregrine Falcons and Other Birds of Prey* (Sherrod, S.K., et al 1982), and in chapter 14 of *Hand-Rearing Birds* (Gage, L. and R. Duerr 2007). See Appendix B for additional reference information.

Rehabilitators using a flight cage, creance flying, falconry training, or evaluating a patient's progress throughout its exercise program, should apprentice under an experienced rehabilitator or falconer. A minimum of six months is recommended for apprenticeship; also recommended is attendance at a skills seminar on the proper use of each technique and methods for evaluating flight parameters. The wildlife rehabilitator should be aware that not all falconers will be able to provide useful instruction in the use of creance flying, as it is used very differently in rehabilitation than in falconry. Even if creance flying is being used, it is strongly recommended that conditioning cages of the referenced size either be used on-site or be found through networking with other rehabilitators or rehabilitation facilities. Raptors in stages immediately prior to release often need more exercise than can be provided on a creance. Movements up to perches, down to food or water, or across to another perch also provide important exercise.

4.4.2 Construction Materials

Outdoor raptor facilities most commonly are constructed of wooden slats and/or solid sheets of wood. Vinyl-coated chain link and vinyl-coated welded wire have been used successfully as roofing material (as long as the mesh is small enough that the bird's head cannot fit through it—i.e., not larger than one-inch), and can be used as an outer wall (outside of vertical barring or heavy netting such as pet screening) as a predator double wall. Other wire should only be used as a double wall outside of vertical slats or as a predator barrier along the bottom of outdoor enclosures. No wire should be used on walls where the bird might be able to cling or climb.

High stress raptors such as kites, falcons, osprey, and accipiters should be housed in facilities adequate to the climate and that eliminate or minimize visual and auditory stress. Solid-sided walls and/or vertical slats with no more than one-inch gaps may be advisable. When secluded cages are not available, or when additional visual occlusion is necessary, translucent material (e.g., bed linens/sheets or shadecloth) may be hung on the outside of the slatted cage. These materials allow some light to enter the enclosure, and slits or holes in the material allow for better ventilation than solid-sided cages.

Depending on the local climate and the construction of an outdoor raptor cage, suitable flooring substrates may include sand, pea gravel, natural dirt, grass, or Astroturf™. Plain concrete, wood chips, hay, straw, and jagged rocks should be avoided. In general, the flooring should be easy to clean and disinfect, and should drain well. As with all species, caging should be cleaned and disinfected between patients.

Flooring of indoor housing should have a removable, disposable, or easily-cleaned covering such as newspaper, bed sheets or similar linens, or Astroturf™.

4.4.3 Furnishings

Raptors require furnishings that are exceptionally sturdy and easily cleaned. All perching substrates must be chosen carefully based on the natural history and size of the species as well as the climate of the area (e.g., hemp or sisal rope rots very quickly in humid environments). Natural limbs (with bark), bow, block, and ring perches are appropriate for certain species of raptors. At least two perches should be placed in each cage, preferably at different heights and different angles. More than one surface substrate should be offered on the perches in each cage, and coverings should be attached such that talons cannot get caught. Perches can be wood doweling or plastic piping (or the equivalent) covered by ¼-inch-pile Astroturf™, Daisy Mat™, hemp, cocomat, or other suitable substrates; ropes should be of natural, untreated material (not synthetic or chemically-treated). Cotton and nylon rope should be avoided as perch covers as they flatten with use, may retain water, and often allow talons to get caught. Perches should have some degree of "give" for landings. Platforms, such as those used for peregrines, can be covered with ¼-inch-pile Astroturf™, Daisy Mat™, cocomat, or other suitable substrates.

[**Editor's Note**: Generic brands of Astroturf™ and Daisy Mat™ are often poorly made, can be easily picked apart and ingested by raptors, and are often difficult to clean. If these types of substates are to be used, they should be of high quality, and ALL perches should be checked daily for unraveling, loose edges, or other potential hazards.]

Raptors with limited or questionable vision, and all raptor orphans not being hacked, need live prey training prior to release. When a raptor has partial or potential vision loss, it is important to test its vision both through its ability to catch live prey and to dodge objects. Because orphans do not have their parents to subsidize them while they learn to hunt, it is important for them to have the opportunity to practice hunting while still in captivity. Therefore, flight cages for these birds should have leaf litter on the ground in which the live prey can hide, and 'trees' in the cage for the birds to maneuver around while in flight. Cages used for live prey testing should be rodent proof, with the lower 2-3 feet of the walls being smooth and solid to prevent rodents escaping. 'Trees' can consist of live trees planted in the cage or in pots within the cage, dead trees, and tree limbs (e.g., used Christmas trees may work for smaller birds), or artificial trees made of poles placed strategically about the cage. All such 'trees' should be moveable so that the position can be changed periodically to challenge the bird.

As for all animals in rehabilitation, appropriate food and adequate drinking water must be provided. Food should be placed in covered areas of the cage and off the ground on stumps, perches, or platforms to prevent ingestion of pea gravel or other substrates, and to minimize potential contamination with soil pathogens and parasites. Provide drinking/bathing water in unlimited activity flight enclosures or even in all cages if appropriate for the bird's medical condition (e.g., a bird with foot wraps or a wing-wrap should not have a bathing/water pan in any cage). Birds without access to drinking water should receive additional water injected into their food. Drinking water, when available, should be easily accessible to minimize disturbance. Pools must be a minimum of 2-6 inches deep and wider than the length of the raptor.

Table 5: Minimum Housing Guidelines for Raptors

Note: This table is not intended to be used independently; it should be used only in conjunction with the information in Chapter 4, Sections 4.1 and 4.4

Order	Restricted Activity (W × L × H)			Limited Activity (W × L × H)			Unlimited Activity (W × L × H)		
	W	L	H	W	L	H	W	L	H
BOOW, BUOW, EASO, ELOW, FEPO, FLOW, NOPO, NSWO, PRSO, WESO, WHSO	12 in 30 cm	17 in 43 cm	12 in 30 cm	3 ft 0.9 m	6 ft 1.8 m	8 ft 2.4 m	8 ft 2.4 m	16 ft 4.9 m	8 ft 2.4 m
AMKE, APFA, EUKE, GRHA, HBKI, MERL, MIKI, **NOHO, NHOW, ROHA, SNKI, SSHA, STHA	16 in 41 cm	23 in 58 cm	19 in 48 cm	6 ft 1.8 m	6 ft 1.8 m	8 ft 2.4 m	8 ft 2.4 m	16 ft 4.9 m	8 ft 2.4 m
BNOW, BWHA, COHA, HWHA, LEOW, RSHA, SEOW, WTKI	20 in 50 cm	27 in 69 cm	22 in 56 cm	6 ft 1.8 m	8 ft 2.4 m	8 ft 2.4 m	10 ft 3.0 m	30 ft 9.1 m	12 ft 3.7 m
BDOW, CBHA, CRCA, GHOW, HRLH, HRSH, NOGO, NOHA, RLHA, RTHA, SPOW, STKI, SWHA, WTHA, ZTHA	20 in 50 cm	27 in 69 cm	24 in 60 cm	6 ft 1.8 m	8 ft 2.4 m	8 ft 2.4 m	10 ft 3.0 m	50 ft 15.2 m	12 ft 3.7 m
BAEA, BLVU, FEHA, GGOW, GOEA, GYFA, OSPR, PEFA, PRFA, **SEEA, SNOW, TUVU, **WTEA	3 ft 0.9 m	3 ft 0.9 m	3 ft 0.9 m	8 ft 2.4 m	10 ft 3.0 m	8 ft 2.4 m	20 ft 6.1 m	100 ft 30.5 m	16 ft 4.9 m

(WxLxH) = Listed in order: Width x Length x Height

* Species are listed using the four letter AOU code (American Ornithologists Union) defined on p. 55

**Indicates that the codes used for these species are not official AOU codes

Codes for Table 5, Raptors

Accipiters
COHA - Cooper's Hawk
NOGO - Northern Goshawk
SSHA - Sharp-shinned Hawk

Medium Buteos
BWHA - Broad-winged Hawk
GRHA - Gray Hawk
ROHA - Roadside Hawk
STHA - Short-tailed Hawk

Large Buteos
CBHA - Common Black Hawk
FEHA - Ferruginous Hawk
HRLH - Harlan's Hawk
HRSH - Harris' Hawk
HWHA - Hawaiian Hawk
RSHA - Red-shouldered Hawk
RTHA - Red-tailed Hawk
RLHA - Rough-legged Hawk
SWHA - Swainson's Hawk
WTHA - White-tailed Hawk
ZTHA - Zone-tailed Hawk

Eagles
BAEA - Bald Eagle
GOEA - Golden Eagle
**WTEA - White-tailed Eagle
**SSEA - Steller's Sea Eagle

Small Falcons
AMKE - American Kestrel
EUKE - Eurasian Kestrel
**NOHO - Northern Hobby
MERL - Merlin

Medium Falcons
APFA - Aplomado Falcon
PEFA - Peregrine Falcon
PRFA - Prairie Falcon

Large Falcons
CRCA - Crested Caracara
GYFA - Gyrfalcon

Harriers
NOHA - Northern Harrier

Kites
HBKI - Hook-billed Kite
MIKI - Mississippi Kite
SNKI - Snail Kite
STKI - Swallow-tailed Kite
WTKI - White-tailed/Black-shouldered Kite

Osprey
OSPR - Osprey

Vultures
BLVU - Black Vulture
TUVU - Turkey Vulture

Small Owls
BOOW - Boreal Owl
BUOW - Burrowing Owl
EASO - Eastern Screech Owl
ELOW - Elf Owl
FEPO - Ferruginous Pygmy Owl
FLOW - Flammulated Owl
NOPO - Northern Pygmy Owl
NSWO - Northern Saw-whet Owl
PRSO - Puerto Rican Screech Owl
WESO - Western Screech Owl
WHSO - Whiskered Screech Owl

Medium Owls
BNOW - Barn Owl
LEOW - Long-eared Owl
NHOW - Northern Hawk Owl
SEOW - Short-eared Owl

Large Owls
BDOW - Barred Owl
GGOW - Great Gray Owl
GHOW - Great Horned owl
SNOW - Snowy Owl
SPOW - Spotted Owl

Chapter 5 – MAMMAL HOUSING REQUIREMENTS

5.1 Overview

General guides for mammal housing are difficult to define due to the variation in size, temperament, and life history in mammals. Obviously, a "one-size- or style-fits-all" approach fails when you are housing mammals from bats to bears. Some principles do apply to all mammal housing, however. For example, double door or similar construction is effective in preventing escapes in outdoor caging. Cage framing material should be placed on the outside of the enclosure with suitable wall material such as wire, wood, or netting on the inside surface. Visual barriers between cages and between humans and cages provide stress relief to all animal patients. Pre-release cages should be isolated and placed in an area similar to release habitat, if possible. All cages should be constructed so that they can be thoroughly cleaned and disinfected regularly.

Most small mammals under four weeks of age can be housed in incubators or aquaria. Small plastic totes, Rubbermaid™-type tubs with wire or other material for proper ventilation, can be used in place of aquaria for eyes-closed infant or young infant mammals. Many rehabilitators have found plastic or rubber containers more cost-effective, plus easier to store and disinfect than glass aquaria. Screen lids with a heavy object placed on top prevent escapes. Heating pads set on low and placed under one-half of the cage or hot water bottles, suitably insulated, should be used to provide heat. A source of humidity should be provided to young animals. Paper towels, tissues, towels, or other suitable materials for nesting areas should be provided. A mirror secured to the side of a cage reduces habituation and allows single animals to see a member of the same species. A rolled sock or toy stuffed animal of appropriate size, with all movable parts removed, can provide security for infants, especially single animals. Juveniles of the same species usually can be housed together if they are no more than one week apart in age, with appropriate increases in housing size. Local regulations may prohibit animals found in different locations from being housed together.

See Chapter 3, "Basic Requirements for Housing Wild Animals in Rehabilitation" for more specific information on general caging considerations when housing mammals.

5.1.1 Materials for Mammal Caging

Indoor caging

Aquaria or hard plastic pet boxes (top openings) work well to house most infant mammals when placed partially on a heating pad set on low or medium (depending on the heating pad and thickness of the box). This type of housing is also recommended for injured adult small mammals (rats, mice, gophers, least weasel, bats, etc.). True neonates of many small mammals can be kept in small cups or boxes inside incubators, aquaria, or totes for the first few days in order to conserve body temperature.

Cardboard carriers or any type of cardboard box is not recommended for housing mammals as cardboard cannot be cleaned and disinfected properly; in addition, holes present in some carriers may present hazards as animals try to crawl through, and gnawing animals will not be securely contained.

Plastic pet carriers and stainless steel or fiberglass veterinary cages are suitable for housing most mid-sized adult mammals (tree squirrels, opossums, woodchucks, raccoon, fox, etc.).

Bedding is necessary for all infant and juvenile mammals and for most adult injured mammals. Bedding must consist of non-raveling materials such as shredded newspaper, towels, or sheets. Terrycloth towels must not be used with small rodents as they can tangle and injure toes, chew, or choke on strands, etc.).

Outdoor caging

Recommended cage sizes provide for necessary square footage (W x L); cage sizes can be altered as long as the square footage remains the same and allows adequate activity for the animal enclosed. Thus, a recommended cage size of 6' x 8' x 6' also could be built as 12' x 4' x 6', as long as a width of 4' allows the animal to move and exercise as needed. Cages are constructed most easily using multiples of the fabricated width or length of the cage material: if using 3' foot wide rolls of wire, cages may be built in 3' increments (e.g., 3' x 3' x 6'); for 4' wide rolls, cages may be built 4' x 8' x 8' or 4' x 4' x 8', etc.). Enclosure design also may vary widely depending on materials used, climatic conditions, species housed, zoning regulations, building permits, and many other considerations. In general, cages should be tall enough to allow a person to walk upright inside the cage, and have enough room for a person to safely maneuver while caring for or catching the animal(s).

Generally walls are made of chain link fencing, welded wire, or wood. When wooden cages are used, they should be water sealed. Avoid using wood (metal is suggested) for the framework of all rodent and lagomorph cages as these animals will gnaw on and destroy wooden surfaces. Welded wire (hardware cloth) of ¼" to ½" (.5 - 1.0 cm) square mesh size is recommended for the outer surface of most small mammal caging to prevent predators (including snakes) from entering and keep infants and small juveniles from escaping (e.g., squirrels and rabbits). 1" x ½" (2 x 1 cm) is recommended for raccoons and larger mammals.

Roofing materials are the same as the walls, with a covered area that provides protection from the elements. Fiberglass is sometimes used on top of the wire to provide protection. Modifications can be made as long as cages remain secure; for example, large raccoon cages and deer pens have been successfully constructed and used that have no roofs, yet still prevent predators from entering and inhabitants from escaping.

A sight barrier such as shadecloth is required around the lower 12" (30 cm) for cottontail rabbits, and around the lower 24" (60 cm) for jack rabbits to minimize visual stimuli that would cause the animals to panic and injure themselves. This type of sight barrier is recommended for all mammal caging to reduce both stress and habituation to humans.

All enclosures should contain a shelter, nestbox, or "hide" appropriate for that species, with the shelter entrance facing away from the cage entrance.

For enclosures built directly on the ground, cage bottoms should be made predator proof either by burying the sides several inches in a concrete border, or by making the walls contiguous with the floor of the cage (either concrete or buried hardware cloth). Larger walk-in mammal cages should have concrete flooring and be sloped for proper drainage. If natural flooring is utilized, wire fencing must be placed under the cage and be covered with a draining gravel (i.e., pea gravel). These types of flooring also prevent burrowing mammals from digging out of the cage and may help to anchor the structure.

For raised enclosures, cage bottoms should be constructed of ¼" hardware cloth to allow for drainage; cage bottoms should be covered by natural substrate such as pine bows or shredded cedar, Astroturf™, rubber mats, Dri-dek™ mats, or similar substrates that will minimize foot damage from the wire and that can be removed for cleaning of the cage.

When possible, all doors should be equipped with a double door system for the protection of the handler and the animal. Whenever possible, the interiors of all outdoor enclosures should attempt to imitate natural habitat/terrain as much as possible. Examples include dirt with raised mounds for burrowing animals, trees or large natural branches for climbing animals, and natural vegetation to provide hides/shelter for all species. Branches should be changed between individuals or groups of animals using the cage. A den should be provided in each cage, with the den entrance facing away from the cage entrance: examples would include a wooden box, fiberglass or plastic animal carrier.

Self-feeders often work well for animals such as raccoons, and may be helpful in reducing habituation to humans.

As mentioned in the General Caging Comments, cages used for raccoons must not be used for any other species due to the high incidence of *Baylisascaris procyonis* (raccoon roundworm) in these animals.

5.2 Special Considerations for Selected Mammals

Since most small mammal young can be housed in the same general manner described above, this section addresses the special housing needs for juvenile and adult mammals (except where noted otherwise). Please refer to Table 6 for specifics regarding cage size.

The order in which the groups of mammals appear below and in Table 6 is based on the standard scientific "evolutionary order" as presented in *A Field Guide to the Mammals of America North of Mexico* (Appendix B, Burt/Grossenheider).

Marsupialia (Opossums):
Hammocks made of one-inch square wire mesh or from burlap sacks, attached to wall or roof (and removable for cleaning); tree limbs and logs at various heights to promote climbing. Plastic barrels for hiding or other things in which to hide (logs, boxes, etc.). Large (ferret-sized) exercise wheels may be used to keep young opossums active.

Chiroptera (Bats):
For bats under rehabilitation, many different considerations are important to proper enclosure construction. Security is of top concern regardless of cage size. For example, most bats can easily escape through a 1/2" x 1" crack. Two different types of caging are necessary to accommodate the differences in the roosting behavior of crevice-dwelling and foliage-roosting bats. Crevice-dwelling bats (free-tailed bats, pallid bats, big browns, silverhaired bats, Myotis bats, evening bats, big-eared bats, and pipistrelles) roost in rock crevices, hollow trees, under bridges, beneath bark and in caves and buildings. Foliage-roosting bats (red bats, Seminole bats, yellow bats, and hoary bats) roost in the open in trees and other vegetation.

Appropriate temperatures for adult bats receiving rehabilitation and infant bats being hand-raised are very important considerations. These temperatures are generally between 90°F - 100°F. A heating pad, set to low, can be attached to one side of the cage to create a temperature gradient. Do not place heating pads on the floor of the container. A bird brooder or a 25-watt red light bulb may be used instead of a heating pad. Place the brooder or light at the top of the cage on the outside. Incubators are inappropriate for bats, as a temperature gradient is needed rather than a constant temperature. Humidity should be provided by use of a humidifier or by keeping a small, damp sponge inside the cage. Padding should be placed on the cage floor to protect injured adults and/or infant bats. Soft fabric allows the bat(s) to climb and hide. Terrycloth is inappropriate due to risk of entanglement.

Caging for crevice-dwelling bats (restricted/limited activity):
All walls and floor of an enclosure should be lined with a soft, snag-resistant fabric such as t-shirt or flannel material. Aquaria, or any sort of hard-sided cage, should be avoided. Adult bats will echolocate when in an unfamiliar setting. When they do this in a hard-sided enclosure, the sound waves bounce back from all sides; the bats realize they are confined, causing unnecessary stress. Use of the smallest-size Reptarium® or a Port-A-Bat® is a better choice. Environmental enrichment can include items made from fabric such as roosting pouches, constructed of a soft non-loop fabric. The addition of ramps or bridges should be constructed from Rubbermaid™ shelf liner or similar product.

Caging for foliage-roosting bats (restricted/limited activity):
Foliage-roosting bats are prone to abrasion-type wing injuries, so they should be encouraged to hang freely rather than cling to the cage side, where they may rub their wings. The cage should be covered with soft, lightweight 1/16" mesh to avoid toe and foot injuries. Port-A-Bats® or Caterpillar Castles® are good choices for housing foliage-roosting species; the mesh is much finer and softer than that of a Reptarium®. A square of Con-Tact® Grip Liner may be attached to the ceiling of the cage; this will encourage the bat to hang freely rather than cling to the cage side. Environmental enrichment should be provided by securely attaching small branches with silk leaves against the ceiling of the cage.

Unlimited activity/mobility flight cages:
Outdoor flight cages should be double enclosed or have a double entry system similar to aviaries. A screened tent with an extra door flap works well for outdoor housing if the area is secure from predators. If a double enclosure is used, the inside cage should be constructed of a frame covered with soft, lightweight 1/16" mesh, netting or nylon screening. One side can be covered with 1/4" mesh to allow insects to enter the enclosure. The outside of the enclosure should be covered with sturdy 1/4"-1/2" metal screening (hardware cloth or hail wire) to protect from predators.

Roosting pouches or boxes should be placed inside flight cages along the ceiling for crevice-dwelling bats. Small branches with silk leaves should be secured along the ceiling for foliage-roosting bats. Hanging plants also work well for shelter and resting areas. A tarp should be placed over a section of the cage to shade the roosting area and to provide shelter against inclement weather.

Water dishes should be small and can be made from baby food jar lids that are placed on the cage floor or film canisters that are cut to one inch high and hung on cage walls (Velcro™ works well to attach these canisters). Small cups can be hung from the sides of the cage for foliage roosting bats; however, marbles or small stones should be placed inside the cup to prevent the bat from falling in and drowning. Food dishes should be placed against cage walls and should be shallow enough to allow bats that self-feed to easily climb in and out, but deep enough to prevent mealworms from escaping. For certain species, such as western pallid bats, food and water should be provided on the ground. Internal light sources used to attract insects should have covered bulbs (plastic, not metal) to prevent bats from having contact with hot light fixtures. Ideally, both a low-wattage incandescent light and a 'black light' (UV) should be provided, as these attract different species of insects.

Environmental enrichment should be included in all caging to provide mental stimulation. Items that are placed into cages to provide diversity should be free of sharp surfaces, easily cleaned, and appropriate for the species.

Transport cages for bats:
Transport carriers should be ventilated, well padded, and covered so they protect and provide a sense of security for the bat inside. They also should be constructed so that they can sit securely inside a vehicle. For example, a screen window can be sewn or glued into a cloth compact-disk carrier (with the plastic insert removed). A seat belt can then be slipped through the handle to secure the carrier during transport.

Ursids (Bears):
Den should be made of solid wood, concrete blocks or bricks, 8'x8'x6'. This will house one adult or two juveniles. Flooring substrate ideally should be natural (dirt and grass) in order to avoid damage to the foot pads. If floors are concrete, ensure that the floor slopes into a drain for cleaning and provide heavy rubber mats to avoid foot damage. Heavy logs and a large indestructible tub for bathing are also necessary.

Procyonids (Raccoons):
Special cage furnishings for this group include hammocks made of half-inch square wire mesh or from burlap sacks, attached to walls or the roof that are removable for cleaning, and plastic barrels or other things in which to hide (e.g., logs). Additionally, tree limbs and logs at various heights to promote climbing should be in enclosures. A wading pool or container applicable to the animal's size should be provided to allow bathing and food handling. Outdoor enclosures should allow 30 square feet per animal when raccoons are group housed. An enclosure which is 12'x18' (216 square feet) could house seven raccoons. Cages used for raccoons should not be used for other species due to possible parasitic infection. Raccoon caging should be constructed of a material that enables it to be flamed or steam-cleaned in order to destroy parasites after each use.

Mustelids (Badgers, Weasels, Skunks, etc.):
This group contains ambitious diggers. The bottom of the cage must be secured so that the animal cannot dig out. A metal garbage can turned on its side and lined with tree trimmings or shavings can be used as a den. A large wooden box with soil should be provided for digging.

Felids (Cats):
Large branches and logs (some hollow) should be provided for climbing, along with high platforms for resting above the cage floor. Other furnishings are plastic barrels or other things to hide in (logs, boxes, etc.).

Marine Mammals:
Shall be housed in accordance with Animal and Plant Health Inspection Service (APHIS) Standards and follow NOAA Fisheries Programmatic Environmental Impact Statement (PEIS) on the Marine Mammal Health and Stranding Response Program (MMHSRP) 2009,

Volume II: Appendix C - Policies and Best Practices for Marine Mammal Stranding Response, Rehabilitation, and Release (Appendix C).

Rodentia (Mice, Rats, Squirrels, etc.):
Generalizations are difficult to make for such a large and diverse group, so refer to the natural history of the species undergoing rehabilitation for a better understanding of appropriate habitat requirements. Placing a heavy object on top of the lid of indoor caging prevents escapes. Paper towel rolls can be used as hiding places. Many small rodents require sand for burrowing and some species may utilize dirt for burying food, dust baths, or other behavioral activities. Various gnawing materials should be included for juveniles five weeks and older. Burrowing can be a very important behavior in this group. Plant material and soil are important habitat requirements for many small mammals. Many species of rodent can chew through plastic or wooden caging, so glass aquaria or wire caging is recommended; wood can be used for framing rodent cages as long as plenty of materials are provided for gnawing (e.g., bone, antlers, fresh branches). Wire for tree squirrels should be 1/2" mesh (1 cm) or smaller.

Outdoor caging should be made of material such as hardware cloth to prevent escape. Dirt or sand floors should have hardware cloth buried along the interior sides and/or the entire botom of the cage, approximately 12" below the surface, to prevent escape. Roofing may be constructed of hardware cloth stapled to wood slats using heavy staples. Branches for gnawing should be included; gnawing curbs tooth growth and is essential; bark on any branches or logs must be edible. Tree squirrels and other climbers require vertical height, and tree squirrels also require horizontal space for jumping. Branches and/or platforms should be provided for climbing enhancements. Nest or den boxes should be included for sleeping and hiding.

Semi-aquatic Mammals (Muskrats, River Otters, Nutria, Beavers):
This group has obvious special needs. Animals must have water containers that are large enough to swim in and are at least two feet deep. Examples include bathtubs, metal troughs, metal or concrete pools (plastic kiddie pools are not deep enough and will be destroyed by the animal). Deep, heavy rubber pans work well for water containers in inside housing. Containers of soil at least one foot (30 cm) deep should be provided for digging, with plastic barrels or other things in which to hide (logs, boxes, etc.) that are attached to the wall of the cage. [Note: Beaver will destroy plastic barrels or other plastic cage furnishing.]

Lagomorpha (Rabbits, Hares, Pikas):
Special construction materials are needed for this group. Avoid using wood in cage construction as these animals will chew through the wood. Avoid using chain link, wire mesh, or hardware cloth as the sole materials in construction of cage walls; these animals do not have good depth perception and will not "see" the fencing. "Sight barriers" at the height of the adult animal's ears (12"-24") made of shade cloth or mesh screening may be used to line the exterior. Do not place cloth or screening on the interior as animals will chew this material. Indoor housing also must be covered to provide visual barriers as a means of reducing stress. If raised, above-ground enclosures are used, the bottom should be constructed of 1/4-inch mesh for drainage, and covered with hay to prevent foot trauma. No protruding objects should be present along the interior surface of cage walls as these animals will usually run the perimeter of their enclosure.

All enclosures should contain a freestanding shelter, facing away from the entrance. A lean-to made of wood or earth is an excellent shelter, especially for jack rabbits, as it affords two exits and prevents the animal from feeling trapped. A carrier placed in the cage may act as a den and facilitate capture if the animals grow accustomed to it and can simply be trapped inside as needed. Natural shrubs, hollow logs, or bales of hay also can be used to provide shade and shelter for rabbits. Branches or logs with edible bark for gnawing to curb tooth growth should be readily available. Jackrabbits grow rapidly in size and strength, requiring large caging by six weeks of age, although they do not wean until 8-12 weeks of age.

Artiodactyla (Hoofed Animals):
Outdoor enclosures are most appropriate when constructed of wood; however, if chain link is used for the walls, drapesor dark shadecloth must be hung over and secured to the inside of the chain link to avoid injury to the animal and to keep it from climbing out (i.e., blankets or tarps tied securely). Circular enclosures work well as animals will be encouraged to run along walls rather than run into a corner and injure themselves. vGeneral practice is to take deer and pronghorn directly from injured adult caging to release in an effort to prevent cage trauma. Bighorn sheep jump high while pronghorn will jump long distances but not as high.

Key to Table 6: Minimum Housing Guidelines for Infant to Juvenile Mammals

(WxLxH) = Listed in order: Width x Length x Height

* = See specific species requirements

(+) = See specific species requirements for hoofed stock

ft = feet

m = meter

in = inch

cm = centimeter

(#) = Number of animals

(L) = Litter - Note: Occassional large litters (8-10 animals) may require larger housing

W = Wire bottom

A = Must have easy access; if not, use larger cage size for safety

** = 12" x 12" x 12" tote can substitute for 10 gal aquarium for Tree Squirrels

Table 6: Minimum Housing Guidelines for Infant to Juvenile Mammals

Note: This table is not intended to be used independently; it should be used only in conjunction with the information in Chapter 5, Sections 5.1 and 5.3

Order/Family	Infant Care (W × L × H)	Nursing/Pre-weaned (W × L × H)	Juvenile Outside (W × L × H)
Marsupialia			
Opossums	10 Gallon / (L) 38 Liter	3 ft × 3 ft × 3 ft / (L) 0.9 m × 0.9 m × 0.9 m	10 ft × 12 ft × 8 ft / (L) 3.0 m × 3.7 m × 2.4 m
Insectivora			
Shrews & Moles	10 Gallon / (L) 38 Liter	20 Gallon / (L) 76 Liter	
Chiroptera (Bats)	6 in × 8 in × 6 in / 15 cm × 20 cm × 15 cm		
Little Browns & Pipistrelles		12 in × 18 in × 12 in / 30 cm × 46 cm × 30 cm	8 ft × 16 ft × 8 ft / 2.4 m × 4.9 m × 2.4 m
Evenings, Reds, Myotis, Big Brown			8 ft × 16 ft × 8 ft / 2.4 m × 4.9 m × 2.4 m
Free-tails, Hoarys, Pallids & Yellows			10 ft × 20 ft × 8 ft / 3.0 m × 6.1 m × 2.4 m
Carnivora			
Bears — Black Bears	20 Gallon / (L) 76 Liter	3 ft × 6 ft × 3 ft / (L) 0.9 m × 1.8 m × 0.9 m	20 ft × 36 ft × 16 ft* / (L) 6.1 m × 11.0 m × 4.9 m
Raccoons, Coatis & Ringtails	10-20 Gallon / (L) 38-76 Liter	3 ft × 3 ft × 3 ft / (3) 0.9 m × 0.9 m × 0.9 m	10 ft × 12 ft × 6 ft / (4) 3.0 m × 3.7 m × 1.8 m
Mustelids			
Martens	10 Gallon / (L) 38 Liter	3 ft × 3 ft × 3 ft / (L) 0.9 m × 0.9 m × 0.9 m	4 ft × 8 ft × 6 ft / (L) 1.2 m × 2.4 m × 1.8 m
Fishers	10 Gallon / (L) 38 Liter	3 ft × 3 ft × 3 ft / (L) 0.9 m × 0.9 m × 0.9 m	6 ft × 8 ft × 6 ft / (L) 1.8 m × 2.4 m × 1.8 m

Minimum Standards for Wildlife Rehabilitation (continued)

Order/Family	Infant Care (W × L × H)	Nursing/Pre-weaned (W × L × H)	Juvenile Outside (W × L × H)
Mustelids (cont'd)			
Weasels & Minks	(L) 10 Gallon / 38 Liter	(L) 10 Gallon / 38 Liter	6 ft × 8 ft × 8 ft (L) 1.8 m × 2.4 m × 2.4 m
River Otters	(L) 20 Gallon / 76 Liter	6 ft × 12 ft × 6 ft (L) 1.8 m × 3.7 m × 1.8 m	6 ft × 12 ft × 6 ft* (L) 1.8 m × 3.7 m × 1.8 m
Sea Otters	(L) 20 Gallon / 76 Liter	6 ft × 12 ft × 6 ft (L) 1.8 m × 3.7 m × 1.8 m	6 ft × 10 ft × 6 ft (L) 1.8 m × 3.0 m × 1.8 m
Wolverines	(1) 10 Gallon / 38 Liter	3 ft × 3 ft × 3 ft (L) 0.9 m × 0.9 m × 0.9 m	8 ft × 12 ft × 6 ft (L) 2.4 m × 3.7 m × 1.8 m
Badgers	(L) 20 Gallon / 76 Liter	3 ft × 3 ft × 3 ft (L) 0.9 m × 0.9 m × 0.9 m	8 ft × 8 ft × 6 ft* (L) 2.4 m × 2.4 m × 1.8 m
Skunks	(L) 20 Gallon / 76 Liter	2 ft × 4 ft × 3 ft (L) 0.6 m × 1.2 m × 0.9 m	10 ft × 12 ft × 6 ft (L) 3.0 m × 3.7 m × 1.8 m
Canids			
Coyotes	(L) 30 Gallon / 114 Liter	3 ft × 3 ft × 3 ft (L) 0.9 m × 0.9 m × 0.9 m	10 ft × 10 ft × 8 ft (L) 3.0 m × 3.0 m × 2.4 m
Wolves	(L) 30 Gallon / 114 Liter	3 ft × 3 ft × 3 ft (L) 0.9 m × 0.9 m × 0.9 m	12 ft × 12 ft × 8 ft (L) 3.7 m × 3.7 m × 2.4 m
Foxes	(L) 30 Gallon / 114 Liter	3 ft × 3 ft × 3 ft (L) 0.9 m × 0.9 m × 0.9 m	4 ft × 4 ft × 8 ft (L) 1.2 m × 1.2 m × 2.4 m
Felids			
Mountain Lions	(L) 10 Gallon / 38 Liter	3 ft × 6 ft × 3 ft (L) 0.9 m × 1.8 m × 0.9 m	8 ft × 24 ft × 8 ft* (L) 2.4 m × 7.3 m × 2.4 m
Bobcats	(L) 10 Gallon / 38 Liter	3 ft × 3 ft × 3 ft (L) 0.9 m × 0.9 m × 0.9 m	10 ft × 10 ft × 8 ft (L) 3.0 m × 3.0 m × 2.4 m
Rodentia			
Large Rodents			
Aplodontia, Marmots, Muskrats, Woodchucks, etc.	(L) 20 Gallon / 76 Liter	4 ft × 4 ft × 3 ft (L) 1.2 m × 1.2 m × 0.9 m	8 ft × 8 ft × 8 ft W (L) 2.4 m × 2.4 m × 2.4 m

Table 6 (cont'd): Minimum Housing Guidelines for Infant to Juvenile Mammals

Order/Family	Infant Care (W × L × H)	Nursing/Pre-weaned (W × L × H)	Juvenile Outside (W × L × H)
Rodentia (cont'd) **Medium Rodents**			
Large/Med Ground Squirrels Prairie Dogs, Rock Squirrels, California Ground Squirrels, etc.	(L) 10 Gallon 38 Liter	(L) 3 ft × 4 ft × 3 ft 0.9 m × 1.2 m × 0.9 m	(L) 6 ft × 8 ft × 8 ft W 1.8 m × 2.4 m × 2.4 m
Small Ground Squirrels 13-Lined, Chipmunks, etc.	(L) 10 Gallon 38 Liter or 6" × 12" × 6" tote	(L) 10-20 Gallon 38-76 Liter or similar cage of 1/2" wire mesh	(L) 3 ft × 6 ft × 6 ft A 0.9 m × 1.8 m × 1.8 m
Tree, Pine & Flying Squirrels	(L) 10-20 Gallon** 38-76 Liter or 12" × 12" × 12" tote	(L) 20 Gallon 76 Liter or 2 ft × 3 ft × 2 ft * or 0.6m × 0.9m × 0.6m or similar cage of 1/2" wire mesh	(L) 8 ft × 8 ft × 8 ft * 2.4 m × 2.4 m × 2.4 m
Pocket Gophers, Voles, Lemmings, Pikas	(L) 10 Gallon 38 Liter or 6" × 12" × 6" tote	(L) 10-20 Gallon 38-76 Liter or similar cage of 1/2" wire mesh	(L) 3 ft × 6 ft × 6 ft A 0.9 m × 1.8 m × 1.8 m
Rats--All	(L) 10 Gallon 38 Liter	(L) 20 Gallon 76 Liter or similar size cage	(L) 3 ft × 6 ft × 6 ft A 0.9 m × 1.8 m × 1.8 m
Mice--All	(L) 10 Gallon 38 Liter	(L) 15-20 Gallon 57-76 Liter	(L) 3 ft × 3 ft × 3 ft 0.9 m × 0.9 m × 0.9 m
Beavers	(L) 20 Gallon 76 Liter	(L) 3 ft × 3 ft × 3 ft 0.9 m × 0.9 m × 0.9 m	(1) 8 ft × 12 ft × 6 ft 2.4 m × 3.7 m × 1.8 m
Porcupines	(L) 15 Gallon 57 Liter	(L) 3 ft × 3 ft × 3 ft 0.9 m × 0.9 m × 0.9 m	(L) 6 ft × 8 ft × 6 ft 1.8 m × 2.4 m × 1.8 m

Order/Family	Infant Care W × L × H	Nursing/Pre-weaned W × L × H	Juvenile Outside W × L × H
Rodentia (cont'd)			
Nutrias	(L) 20 Gallon / 76 Liter	(L) 2 ft × 4 ft × 3 ft / 0.6 m × 1.2 m × 0.9 m	(L) 6 ft × 8 ft × 6 ft / 1.8 m × 2.4 m × 1.8 m
Lagomorpha			
Jackrabbits	(1) 20 Gallon / 76 Liter		(L) 20 ft × 20 ft × 6 ft / 6.1 m × 6.1 m × 1.8 m
(2-6 weeks)		18 in × 18 in × 12 in / 46 cm × 46 cm × 30 cm	
(6-12 weeks)		10 ft × 10 ft × 4 ft / 3.0 m × 3.0 m × 1.2 m	
Cottontail Rabbits	(L) 10 Gallon / 38 Liter	(L) 10 Gallon / 38 Liter	(L) 6 ft × 6 ft × 4 ft / 1.8 m × 1.8 m × 1.2 m
Artiodactyla			
Wild Pigs	(L) 2 ft × 2 ft × 2 ft / 0.6 m × 0.6 m × 0.6 m	(L) 10 ft × 15 ft × 8 ft / 3.0 m × 4.6 m × 2.4 m	(L) 10 ft × 15 ft × 8 ft / 3.0 m × 4.6 m × 2.4 m
Elk	(1-2) 6 ft × 6 ft × 2 ft / 1.8 m × 1.8 m × 0.6 m	(4) 12 ft × 20 ft × 6 ft / 3.7 m × 6.1 m × 1.8 m	(6) 50 ft × 80 ft × 8 ft (+) / 15.2 m × 24.4 m × 2.4 m (+)
Deer	(1-2) 4 ft × 4 ft × 2 ft / 1.2 m × 1.2 m × 0.6 m	(4) 10 ft × 15 ft × 6 ft / 3.0 m × 4.6 m × 1.8 m	(6) 30 ft × 50 ft × 8 ft (+) / 9.1 m × 15.2 m × 2.4 m (+)
Pronghorns	(1-2) 4 ft × 4 ft × 2 ft / 1.2 m × 1.2 m × 0.6 m	(4) 10 ft × 15 ft × 6 ft / 3.0 m × 4.6 m × 1.8 m	(+)
Bighorn Sheep	(1-2) 4 ft × 4 ft × 2 ft / 1.2 m × 1.2 m × 0.6 m	(4) 10 ft × 15 ft × 6 ft / 3.0 m × 4.6 m × 1.8 m	(6) 30 ft × 50 ft × 8 ft / 9.1 m × 15.2 m × 2.4 m
Xenartha			
Armadillos	(L) 15 Gallon / 57 Liter	(L) 3 ft × 3 ft × 3 ft / 0.9 m × 0.9 m × 0.9 m	(L) 6 ft × 8 ft × 6 ft / 1.8 m × 2.4 m × 1.8 m

Table 7: Minimum Housing Guidelines for Adult or Adult-sized Mammals

Note: This table is not intended to be used independently; it should be used only in conjunction with the information in Chapter 4, Sections 4.1 and 4.3

Order/Family	Adult Outside (W x L x H)	Restricted Injured Adult (W x L x H)
Marsupialia		
Opossums	(1) 4 ft x 4 ft x 8 ft / 1.2 m x 1.2 m x 2.4 m	(1) 2 ft x 2 ft x 2 ft / 0.6 m x 0.6 m x 0.6 m
Insectivora		
Shrews & Moles		(1) 10 Gallon / 38 Liter
Chiroptera (Bats)		12 in x 18 in x 12 in / 30 cm x 46 cm x 30 cm
Little Browns & Pipistrelles	8 ft x 16 ft x 8 ft / 2.4 m x 4.8 m x 2.4 m	
Evenings, Reds, Myotis Big Browns,	8 ft x 16 ft x 8 ft / 2.4 m x 4.8 m x 2.4 m	
Free-tails, Hoarys, Pallids & Yellows	10 ft x 20 ft x 8 ft / 3.0 m x 6.1 m x 2.4 m	
Carnivora		
Bears — Black Bears	(1) 20 ft x 36 ft x 16 ft * / 6.1 m x 11.0 m x 4.9 m	(1) 8 ft x 12 ft x 8 ft / 2.4 m x 3.7 m x 2.4 m
Raccoons, Coatis & Ringtails	(1) 10 ft x 12 ft x 8 ft / 3.0 m x 3.7 m x 2.4 m	(1) 2 ft x 3 ft x 3 ft / 0.6 m x 0.9 m x 0.9 m
Mustelids		
Martens	(1) 4 ft x 8 ft x 8 ft / 1.2 m x 2.4 m x 2.4 m	(1) 2 ft x 2 ft x 2 ft / 0.6 m x 0.6 m x 0.6 m
Fishers	(1) 6 ft x 8 ft x 8 ft / 1.8 m x 2.4 m x 2.4 m	(1) 4 ft x 3 ft x 3 ft / 1.2 m x 0.9 m x 0.9 m
Weasels & Minks	(1) 6 ft x 8 ft x 6 ft / 1.8 m x 2.4 m x 1.8 m	(1) 3 ft x 3 ft x 3 ft / 0.9 m x 0.9 m x 0.9 m
River Otters	(1) 6 ft x 12 ft x 6 ft * / 1.8 m x 3.7 m x 1.8 m	(1) 4 ft x 3 ft x 3 ft * / 1.2 m x 0.9 m x 0.9 m
Sea Otters	(1) 6 ft x 12 ft x 6 ft / 1.8 m x 3.7 m x 1.8 m	(1) 6 ft x 8 ft x 6 ft / 1.8 m x 2.4 m x 1.8 m
Wolverines	(1) 10 ft x 12 ft x 6 ft / 3.0 m x 3.7 m x 1.8 m	(1) 4 ft x 3 ft x 3 ft / 1.2 m x 0.9 m x 0.9 m
Badgers	(1) 10 ft x 12 ft x 6 ft * / 3.0 m x 3.7 m x 1.8 m	(1) 3 ft x 3 ft x 3 ft / 0.9 m x 0.9 m x 0.9 m
Skunks	(1) 8 ft x 10 ft x 6 ft / 2.4 m x 3.0 m x 1.8 m	(1) 3 ft x 3 ft x 3 ft / 0.9 m x 0.9 m x 0.9 m

Order/Family	Adult Outside			Injured Adult Restricted		
	W x	L x	H	W x	L x	H
Canids						
Coyotes	(1) 10 ft x 3.0 m x	10 ft x 3.0 m x	8 ft 2.4 m	(1) 3 ft x 0.9 m x	3 ft x 0.9 m x	3 ft 0.9 m
Wolves	(1) 12 ft x 3.6 m x	12 ft x 3.6 m x	8 ft 2.4 m	(1) 4 ft x 1.2 m x	3 ft x 0.9 m x	3 ft 0.9 m
Foxes	(1) 6 ft x 1.8 m x	6 ft x 1.8 m x	8 ft 2.4 m	(1) 3 ft x 0.9 m x	3 ft x 0.9 m x	3 ft 0.9 m
Felids						
Mountain Lions	(1) 8 ft x 2.4 m x	24 ft x 7.3 m x	8 ft * 2.4 m	(1) 4 ft x 1.2 m x	3 ft x 0.9 m x	3 ft 0.9 m
Bobcats	(1) 10 ft x 3.0 m x	10 ft x 3.0 m x	8 ft 2.4 m	(1) 3 ft x 0.9 m x	3 ft x 0.9 m x	3 ft 0.9 m
Rodentia						
Large Rodents Aplodontia, Marmots, Muskrats, Woodchucks, etc.	(1) 8 ft x 2.4 m x	8 ft x 2.4 m x	8 ft W 2.4 m	(1) 3 ft x 0.9 m x	3 ft x 0.9 m x	2 ft 0.6 m
Large/Medium Ground Squirrels Prairie Dogs, Rock Sqs, Calfornia Ground Sqs, etc.	(1) 6 ft x 1.8 m x	8 ft x 2.4 m x	6 ft 1.8 m	(1) 2 ft x 0.6 m x	3 ft x 0.9 m x	2 ft 0.6 m
Small Ground Squirrels 13-lined, Chipmunks, etc.	(1) 6 ft x 1.8 m x	8 ft x 2.4 m x	6 ft 1.8 m	(1) 1 ft x 0.3 m x	1 ft x 0.3 m x	1 ft 0.3 m
Tree Squirrels	(1) 8 ft x 2.4 m x	8 ft x 2.4 m x	8 ft * 2.4 m	(1) 2 ft x 0.6 m x	3 ft x 0.9 m x	2 ft 0.6 m
Pine & Flying Squirrels	(1) 8 ft x 2.4 m x	8 ft x 2.4 m x	8 ft * 2.4 m	(1) 1 ft x 0.3 m x	1 ft x 0.6 m x	1 ft 0.3 m
Pocket Gophers, Voles, Lemmings, Pikas	(1) 3 ft x 0.9 m x or 3 ft x	4 ft x 1.2 m x 6 ft x	3 ft 0.9 m A 6 ft	(1) 1 ft x 0.3 m x	1 ft x 0.3 m x	1 ft 0.3 m
Rats -- All	(1) 3 ft x 0.9 m x	4 ft x 1.2 m x	3 ft 0.9 m	(1) 10 Gallon 38 Liter		
Mice -- All	(1) 2 ft x 0.6 m x	2 ft x 0.6 m x	2 ft 0.6 m	(1) 10 Gallon 38 Liter		
Beavers	(1) 8 ft x 2.4 m x	12 ft x 3.7 m x	6 ft 1.8 m	(1) 4 ft x 1.2 m x	3 ft x 0.9 m x	3 ft 0.9 m
Porcupines	(1) 6 ft x 1.8 m x	8 ft x 2.4 m x	8 ft 2.4 m	(1) 3 ft x 0.9 m x	3 ft x 0.9 m x	3 ft 0.9 m
Nutrias	(1) 6 ft x 1.8 m x	8 ft x 2.4 m x	6 ft 1.8 m	(1) 3 ft x 0.9 m x	3 ft x 0.9 m x	3 ft 0.9 m

Order/Family	Adult Outside			Restricted Injured Adult		
	W x L x H			W x L x H		
Lagomorpha						
Jackrabbits	(1)	20 ft x 20 ft x 6 ft 6.1 m x 6.1 m x 2.4 m		(1)	18 in x 36 in x 12 in 46 cm x 91 cm x 30 cm	
Cottontail Rabbits	(1)	6 ft x 6 ft x 6 ft 1.8 m x 1.8 m x 1.8 m		(1)	12 in x 18 in x 12 in 30 cm x 46 cm x 30 cm	
Artiodactyla						
Wild Pigs	(1)	10 ft x 15 ft x 8 ft 3.0 m x 4.6 m x 2.4 m				
Elk	(6)	50 ft x 80 ft x 8 ft 15.2 m x 24.3 m x 2.4 m	(+)			
Deer	(6)	30 ft x 50 ft x 8 ft 9.1 m x 15.2 m x 2.4 m	(+)			
Pronghorns	(+)					
Bighorn Sheep	(6)	30 ft x 50 ft x 8 ft 9.1 m x 15.2 m x 2.4 m				
Xenartha						
Armadillos	(L)	6 ft x 8 ft x 4 ft 1.8 m x 2.4 m x 1.2 m				

(WxLxH) = Listed in order: Width x Length x Height

* = See specific species requirements

(+) = See specific species requirements for hoofed stock

ft = feet

m = meter

in = inch

cm = centimeter

(#) = Number of animals

W = Wire bottom

A = Must have easy access; if not, use larger cage size for safety

** = 12" x 12" x 12" tote can substitute for 10 gal aquarium for Tree Squirrels

Chapter 6 – REPTILE HOUSING REQUIREMENTS

6.1 General Reptile Housing Considerations

Reptiles are a diverse group consisting of lizards, snakes, turtles, tortoises, alligators, and crocodiles. With over 300 species of reptiles in the United States and Canada, it is impossible to cover the requirements of each species in this paper. However, these guidelines have been developed as minimums to keep an animal healthy and reasonably content in temporary captive situations and are suitable for animals undergoing rehabilitation.

It is essential to learn the habits of a particular species and apply that knowledge to the size, lighting, heating, furnishings, and substrate of the enclosure. However, all reptile enclosures must:

- be large enough to provide a thermal gradient
- have good quality full-spectrum light with a photoperiod suitable for the species, or have access to natural sunlight outdoors (sunlight through glass windows is not full-spectrum)
- provide humidity levels appropriate for the species
- have fresh drinking/bathing water available at all times
- have good ventilation and drainage
- be escape proof (lockable for snakes)
- have hide boxes where the animal can feel secure—one in the warm end and one in the cool end
- have an illumination gradient so animals can choose different levels of light
- approximate the natural environment of that species to encourage normal behaviors such as swimming, basking, burrowing, foraging, hunting, climbing, or any other activity necessary for the well-being of the animal

The cage sizes in Table 7 are the *minimum* sizes to be used; many of the species require larger enclosures because of activity levels and behavioral needs. For example, a snake species that pursues prey would require more space than one that ambushes prey. Conversely, reptiles with restricted activity or mobility (such as severe injuries or surgical limitations) may be kept temporarily in smaller enclosures before moving into larger recovery quarters. Further, some reptiles may have special keeping requirements that these recommendations will not cover adequately.

However, no reptile should be housed in an enclosure less than two feet long by one foot wide (61 by 30.5 cm). It is impossible to provide a proper temperature gradient and room for exercise in an enclosure smaller than these measurements.

Reptiles are best kept alone during the rehabilitation process. Unlike birds and mammals, most reptiles lead solitary lives and do not need or want the company of others. Housing them individually eliminates the stress of competing for resources, stops the spread of disease, and prevents injuries. Keeping reptiles as lone animals is the safest course during rehabilitation, both physically and psychologically.

6.2 Special Considerations for Aquatic Turtles

For aquatic turtle habitats, external canister filters such as the Eheim® are absolutely necessary to maintain water quality. They are extremely reliable, easy to start and clean, and have replaceable parts. Most filters are sized according to the filtration needs of fish. Turtles put out much more waste, so increase the size of the filter. For example, with a 50 gallon (190 liter) tank, use a filter rated for at least 100 gallons (380 liters). Even with filtration, however, regular water changes are still essential. Fifty percent of the water should be changed every week and a complete water change should be done monthly. If injuries require shallow water that cannot be filtered, the water must be changed at least once a day.

Water depth for aquatic turtles must be deeper than the turtle is wide to allow for complete submersion. This allows a turtle to easily right itself if it should become overturned in the water.

All aquatic turtles must have a large, stable basking area that allows the turtle to get completely out of the water and dry off to prevent shell rot, skin infections, and other medical issues. Floating pieces of cork are not recommended for basking areas since most are not large or strong enough to support an adult turtle. One idea for a basking platform is to glue (using aquarium glue) pieces of rigid tubing to the sides of the tank just above the water level and rest a platform on the tubes. A ramp must be added so the turtle can climb up to the platform. Use caution with rocks as turtles can move them and possibily be trapped and drown.

6.3 Construction Materials

Aquariums or terrariums work for housing some reptile species, depending on the size and environmental requirements of the animal. Clear glass, however, can increase stress since the reptile is exposed to human movements and most reptiles perceive humans as predators. To reduce stress, cover the glass with a towel or sheet, or tape cardboard to the sides.

Glass aquariums are *not* appropriate for semi-aquatic turtles, box turtles, or tortoises. For these species, aquariums increase stress and even contribute to health problems due to poor air circulation, and lack of space for exercise, microclimates, and temperature gradients.

Appropriate housing choices include large plastic storage containers, pre-formed ponds, cement-mixing tubs, and livestock feeding and watering tubs. These containers are inexpensive, easy to handle and clean, stack for storage, and come in a wide variety of sizes. The caging must be secure to prevent escape and/or injury to the animal or to other animals in the facility. The caging must be free of rough surfaces, and must be furnished appropriately for the species.

If animals are housed outdoors, part of the enclosure must be covered with shadecloth to provide protection from the sun. Never use glass aquariums outdoors as these can quickly overheat and cause the death of the animal.

6.4 Lighting

Correct lighting is important for both the physical and psychological health of reptiles in captivity. The best type of light is natural sunlight in an outside environment. However, injuries or illness may prevent keeping reptiles outside. Therefore, indoor artificial lighting must duplicate the type, intensity, and photoperiod of natural sunlight as closely as possible to stimulate normal behavior, including basking and eating.

Artificial lighting must have adequate levels of UVA, which affects the way reptiles visualize food, and UVB to stimulate production of Vitamin D3, which is necessary to metabolize calcium.

Two other factors are equally important in choosing the correct artificial lighting. One is the color rendering index (CRI), which refers to how well a light source shows the true colors of an object. Many reptiles rely on color for feeding purposes and correct CRI may aid in appetite stimulation. Lights with a CRI of 80 to 90 are appropriate for reptiles and amphibians. The other is color temperature, which describes the apparent warmth or coolness of a light source. The preferred color temperature to mimic midday sunlight is from 5,000 to 5,500°K (degrees Kelvin). This natural color temperature stimulates normal activity and feeding patterns in captive reptiles and amphibians.

There are many types of lights marketed for reptiles. Be aware that not all bulbs supply the elements required for good lighting. UV light bulbs and tubes are constantly being improved. To learn about the latest products, see the website at < http://www.uvguide.co.uk >, which is dedicated to researching the use of ultraviolet light in reptile husbandry.

Enclosures should have an illumination gradient. Areas of bright light must be balanced with areas shielded from the light. Depending on the species, these areas can be heavily planted, or contain hide boxes or burrows.

Many reptiles obtain physiological cues from light/dark cycles. Light intensity and photoperiod have been shown to have an effect on hormone and neurotransmitter activity in reptiles, which can impact food intake, stress levels, reproduction, wound healing, and normal behavior. Photoperiods of 12 to 14 hours meet the light requirements of most reptiles. Lights should be on timers to ensure that the photoperiod is consistent. All lights must be turned off at night.

6.5 Heating

Reptiles are ectotherms, meaning they depend on external sources to regulate their body temperature. Proper temperatures are essential for their metabolic processes to function. Each species has a preferred optimal temperature zone required for the animal to be able to digest food, maintain bodily functions, metabolize medications, and recover from injuries. Reptiles maintain body temperature through behavioral choices—basking on a log, burrowing into leaf litter, entering or leaving water, or, in some cases, changing color or body shape to increase or decrease heat uptake.

The key term to remember when heating a reptile enclosure is *thermal gradient*. The thermal gradient provides a range of temperatures encompassing the preferred temperatures of a particular species. The gradient is achieved by having a cool area at one end of the enclosure, a warmer area at the other end, and a localized basking spot with the highest temperature. It is impossible to judge a thermal gradient by feel, so always use two thermometers to monitor the temperature in an enclosure—one at the cool end and one at the warm end. Enclosures must be large enough to permit a temperature gradient so reptiles can regulate their body temperatures by moving away from or toward the warmth.

Reptiles have evolved to raise their body temperature by basking in the sun. They associate light from the sun above them with the heat source. Basking spots should have both a full spectrum light for UVB exposure and a heat source (which can be an ordinary incandescent light bulb). For safety, make sure that neither the reptile nor any substrate can directly contact the heat source.

The type of animal determines how heat is provided. Turtles and most lizards place themselves in direct sunlight to warm up. Other species, including most snakes and some lizards, increase their body temperature by contact with warm surfaces, so a flat rock should be placed under the basking light. The rock will absorb the heat and allow the reptile to warm itself. Electric hot rocks are not recommended; they have heating elements that can be unstable and reach temperatures that cause severe burns.

When combined with UV lights, ceramic heat emitters are excellent for providing heat for basking during the day. Since these heating elements emit no light, they also can be used if additional warmth is needed at night after the lights are turned off. Ceramic heat emitters get very hot and should be installed in heat-resistant porcelain sockets with wire guards.

Use heating pads with caution. Heating pads provide little direct radiant heat and can seriously impair thermoregulatory behavior in many species. They should be avoided as the sole heat source as they do not encourage natural basking. Healthy reptiles, or those that have already recovered from critical situations, do not need heating pads. Many species burrow to avoid heat, so heat provided from the bottom of the cage is counterproductive. Heating pads can, however, be useful for warming reptiles with respiratory diseases, or those on antibiotic therapy where body temperature needs to be maintained within close tolerances to attain maximum drug effectiveness.

Once a reptile is past the critical stage, enclosure temperatures should drop slightly at night. The night temperatures will vary depending on species, but usually not below 65°F (18°C) for US temperate species. This nightly temperature drop reduces stress by exposing the animal to the natural temperature fluctuation it normally experiences in the wild.

Careful observation will help to adjust temperatures for the optimum well-being of the animals. A reptile should move about the enclosure to regulate their temperature. If an animal spends all of its time under the basking light, the enclosure may be too cold. Conversely, if the animal never goes near the basking area, the enclosure may be too warm.

Aquatic turtles also need a thermal gradient: water is the cool area, the ambient air on their dry basking platforms is the warm area, and the localized basking spot on the platform is the warmest area. Submersible aquarium heaters can be used to warm the water in aquatic or semi-aquatic enclosures, if necessary. These heaters must have guards or cages to prevent breakage and to keep animals from contacting them.

The following are _general_ temperature guidelines for a sampling of species. Rehabilitators are encouraged to research the _specific_ needs for species in their area.

Turtles:

Box turtles - temperature gradient of 70° F (21° C) at the cool end ranging to 85° F (29.5° C) in the warm end, with a 88° F (31° C) in the basking area.

Warm aquatic turtles - e.g., sliders (*Trachemys scripta*), cooters (*Pseudemys* sp.), painted turtles (*Chrysemys picta*), common map (*Graptemys geographica*): water temperatures 76° F (24.5° C). A heat source over one section of the basking platform should provide a basking temperature of 88° F (31° C).

Cool aquatic turtles - e.g., common musk (*Stenotherus odoratus*), Eastern mud (*Kinosternon subrubrum*), spotted (*Clemmys guttata*), common snapper (*Chelydra serpentine*): these species prefer cooler water temperatures around 73° F (23° C), with a basking area around 88° F (31° C).

Snakes:

King (*Lampropeltis* sp.), gopher, bull, and pine (*Pituophis* sp.), rat (*Elaphe obsoleta*), corn (*Elaphe guttata*): 70° to 75° F (21° to 24° C) in the cool end to 85° F (29.5° C) in the warm end with a localized basking area around 88° F (31° C).

Lizards:

Great Plains skinks (*Eumeces obsoletus*) - temperature gradient from 78° F (25.5° C) in the cool end to 86°F (30°C) in the warm end, with a basking area of 95° F (35° C).

Eastern fence lizard (*Sceloporus undulates*) - 71° F (21.5° C) in the cool end to 86° F (30° C) in the warm end, with a basking spot of 90° F (32° C).

6.6 Humidity

Humidity is another factor to be considered in housing reptiles. Just supplying a water bowl is not enough to maintain the humidity necessary for the turtle's good health. Box turtles, for example, require a *minimum* relative humidity of 51% to maintain activity and health. A humidity gauge (easily purchased online or in a pet store) can be used to monitor humidity levels in the enclosure. Depending on species, humidity can be locally increased by using areas of moist substrate and by creating humid burrows and hiding areas.

Humidity is also important for healthy skin in snakes. Temperate species do well with humidity around 40 to 60%. Monitor humidity carefully—less than 35% makes it difficult for snakes to shed and also can crack and flake scales; more than 70% can lead to ulcerative dermatitis.

Always give reptiles control over their environment through temperature and moisture gradients. When reptiles are forced to be too hot or too cold, too dry or too wet, it contributes to the stress level. When comfortable in the environment and able to make choices for heat and humidity regulation, reptiles will thrive.

6.7 Furnishings

Cage accessories contribute to an animal's mental and physical health by providing a stimulating and enriched environment. Enrichment increases the well-being of captive animals by reducing stress, inducing exercise, providing stimulation, and allowing for natural behaviors. To provide environmental enrichment, it is essential to understand the natural behavior of the animal. For example, rat and corn snakes (*Elaphe* spp.) are climbers, so branches and vines are necessary for their enclosure. Chuckwallas (*Sauromalus* spp.) are rock dwellers that require rocky crevices for security. Desert iguanas (*Dipsosaurus dorsalis*) are both burrowers and climbers that need branches for climbing and PVC pipes set on an angle in the substrate to form burrows.

Reptile furnishings must include:

- Hide boxes—All reptiles must be allowed to hide and placing suitably sized hide boxes at both ends of the cage is usually adequate to support the need for a sense of safety. Snakes also need a humidity box to aid in the shedding process. The box can be made from an opaque plastic container with an access hole cut in the side. Make it just large enough to fit the loosely coiled snake and place a layer of moist sphagnum moss inside.

- Rocks, plants, or branches—as appropriate for the species.
  - Positioning a large, flat rock or pile of rocks in which the animal can hide offers security and an opportunity to engage in normal hunting behavior. For example, rosy boas (*Charina trivirgata*) conceal themselves beneath overhanging rocks or in crevices and wait in ambush for prey. Make sure all rock piles are secure by using aquarium glue to hold formations together for stability.
  - Any species that climbs should be given a selection of branches, vines, and rocks to encourage that behavior. Create different levels of climbing or basking branches to increase useable space in the enclosure.
  - A rough rock or piece of wood bark should be placed in snake enclosures to allow snakes to rub against it and assist in skin shedding. Plastic plants placed in aquatic turtle habitats offer security and resting places; live plants provide food.

- Water—Fresh water always must be available. Water bowls must be large enough for the reptile to fit its entire body into to soak and drink. Shallow stainless steel puppy feeding pans from 8 to 12 inches (20 to 30.5 cm) in diameter make great water bowls for many reptiles, especially box turtles. For desert dwellers, keep the water in the cooler end of the habitat to avoid increasing the humidity to uncomfortable levels. Some lizards, such as the green anole (*Anolis carolinensis*) will not drink from standing water; the cage must be misted so they can lap water off leaves and other surfaces.

6.7.1 Substrates

Selection of an appropriate substrate is extremely important to the long-term health of any reptile. Substrate is one element of creating a microclimate that is essential to many reptile species, especially those that require substrates for burrowing and thermoregulation. Box turtles, for example, require a deep layer of leaf litter, sphagnum moss, and soil. They bury themselves in the substrate to maintain the humidity necessary for their good health.

Substrates may change as the reptile moves through the rehabilitation process. For example, a severely injured animal can be kept on towels for a time, then moved to a more natural substrate as it recovers.

For tactile stimulation and digging opportunities, use multiple species-appropriate substrates of varying depths and moisture levels. Below are a few substrate choices. (Note: Not all substrates are good for every reptile—know the precise requirements of your animals.)

Caution: If using any particulate substrate, food should be placed on a piece of flat rock, slate, or a plate so none of the substrate is ingested.

Aspen—Recommended for snakes from arid climates. Can be mixed with leaf litter for other snakes. The shredded type is absorbent, nonabrasive, and lacks the volatiles that make so many tree-chip products unsuitable. Not recommended for turtles or tortoises.

Astroturf™—Acceptable for some snakes. Several pieces, cut to fit the enclosure should be kept at all times. Since it is not absorbent, it should be changed when soiled; loose strings should be trimmed regularly as the material wears. Not recommended for lizards and turtles that may catch and tear their claws in the fabric and loose strings.

Coco fiber (e.g., Bed-a-Beast®)—Shredded coconut fiber sold in "bricks" and expands when completely soaked. Can be mixed with other substrate such as soil and leaf litter. Good for high humidity species.

Cypress mulch—Natural looking and good for species requiring high humidity.

Gravel—Can be used in aquatic turtle habitats to encourage natural behaviors such as food foraging. Gravel should be large enough so the turtle cannot ingest it. Gravel should be smooth, with no sharp edges. It can be washed, disinfected with bleach, rinsed well, sun-dried, and reused.

Leaf litter—Great alone or mixed with soil and/or sphagnum.

Mulch—May be used if it contains no cedar, pine, or similar wood. Check the mulch before buying; if it smells 'piney' it contains potentially harmful volatiles.

Sand—Should be limited to those animals that habitually live in sand dunes or desert areas, or as a water substrate for species such as soft-shelled turtles. Play sand is less abrasive and safer than other varieties.

Soil—Should be sterilized before use. If using potting soil, make sure it contains no perlite, vermiculite, fertilizers, or chemicals.

Sphagnum moss (not peat moss)—Long fiber sphagnum moss can be used for many species, especially burrowing animals. Mixed with leaf litter and soil, this makes an excellent substrate for box turtles and for the land area of semi-aquatics like wood turtles. The material should be turned over periodically to spread moisture that may collect within the moss.

Towels—Are easily cleaned and disinfected by machine washing in hot water, soap, and bleach. They are especially suited for injured reptiles that cannot be kept on a more natural substrate. Towels may be moistened to raise ambient humidity and provide a humid hiding area.

The following substrates are **not recommended:**

Calci-sand—**not recommended.** Implicated in impactions and eye irritation.

Carefresh™—**not recommended.** Dry, dusty, and has been implicated in respiratory infections.

Cedar—**not recommended.** It contains volatile oils that are toxic to reptiles.

Clay—**not recommended.** Often used for kitty litter, it should never be used as a substrate. It is extremely dehydrating and can cause respiratory problems, skin problems, and prevent snakes from shedding properly.

Corncob—**not recommended.** It is easily ingested and may cause intestinal impaction.

Kitty Litter—see Clay

Newspaper—**not recommended.** Although it is cheap and easy to clean, it does not supply a microclimate. It is too dry for many species, especially box turtles. It also prevents many species from engaging in normal behaviors.

Paper Toweling—**not recommended** for the same reasons as newspaper.

Peat—**not recommended**, as it is dusty, dries easily and may irritate reptile mucosa; can also cause respiratory ailments.

Pine or redwood bark or mulch—**not recommended.** These woods contain resins that are toxic to the nervous system of reptiles.

Rabbit pellets—**not recommended.** Molds quickly when wet and can cause eye and respiratory problems. These pellets are also difficult to walk on and can lead to deformities in hatchlings of certain species.

Table 8: Minimum Housing Guidelines for Reptiles

Note: This table is not intended to be used independently; it should be used only in conjunction with the information in Chapter 6, Sections 6.1 through 6.3

Note: All snake and lizard enclosures should have a cover to prevent escape.
6" = 15 cm, 12" = 30 cm, 24" = 60 cm

<u>Type</u>	<u>Length</u>	<u>Width</u>	<u>Height</u>
Snakes			
Burrowing	3/4 animal's length (not less than 24")	1/3 animal's length (not less than 12")	3/4 animal's length, not less than 12" add 6" to 12" for substrate
Terrestrial	3/4 animal's length (not less than 24")	1/3 animal's length (not less than 12")	3/4 animal's length, not less than 12"
Semi-aquatic	1.5 animal's length (not less than 24")	animal's length (not less than 12")	3/4 animal's length not less than 12"
Arboreal types	3/4 animal's length (not less than 24")	1/3 animal's length (not less than 12")	animal's length, not less than 12"
Lizards			
Burrowing	3 x animal's length (not less than 24")	2x animal's length (not less than 12")	animal's length add 6" to 12" for substrate
Terrestrial	3 x animal's length (not less than 24")	2 x animal's length (not less than 12")	animal's length or high enough to prevent escape
Semi-Aquatic	3 x animal's length (not less than 24")	2 x animal's length (not less than 12")	animal's length or high enough to prevent escape, plus 12" to 24" for water depth
Arboreal types	3 x animal's length (not less than 24")	2 x animal's length (not less than 12")	2 - 3 x animal's length
Crocodilians	5 x animal's length	2 x animal's length	high enough to prevent escape
Turtles			
Terrestrial	5 x animal's length (not less than 24")	3 x animal's length (not less than 12")	high enough to prevent escape, usually 2 x carapace length
Aquatic and Semi-Aquatic	5 x animal's length (not less than 24")	3 x animal's length (not less than 12")	high enough to prevent escape, plus water to a depth 2 x animal's width

Chapter 7 – FINAL DISPOSITION

7.1 Overview

Once an animal comes into rehabilitation, it is faced with one of four fates; death from its injuries, permanent confinement as an education or placed animal due to factors preventing release, successful rehabilitation and release, or euthanasia. Determining the suitability of an animal for permanent confinement is addressed elsewhere (Appendix C). This chapter addresses the last two outcomes—release and euthanasia. Both are complex tasks for the rehabilitator. Successful release of a rehabilitated animal is predicated on an understanding of biological and non-biological factors. These factors include medical, behavioral and physical readiness of the animal, life stage, release strategy, and release habitat.

Euthanasia is perhaps the hardest task a rehabilitator has to perform. Animals should not be considered for release that have vision impaired in both eyes, have amputated wings or legs, are imprinted, have a high likelihood of infecting wild animals with disease, or are rabies vector species from an area in which rabies is endemic (unless dictated otherwise by a local RVS rehabilitation program—see Section 2.3.3). Some species specific reasons exist to preclude the release of some animals, such as the loss of incisors in rodents, the loss of a tail in those species using a tail for balance or warmth, and the loss of opposing digits in those raptors using their talons to acquire food. Other reasons exist that animals should not be released as well. These animals may find freedom through euthanasia.

7.2 Minimum Standards for Release of Wildlife Following Rehabilitation

Establishing and following set guidelines for release condition will aid in initial decisions for treatment, husbandry care protocols, and evaluation of readiness for release. For all wild animals undergoing rehabilitation, the following criteria must be met prior to release.

A brief physical exam should be performed to ensure that the patient is healthy and ready for release. In general, candidates for release must:

- Exhibit full recovery from the original injury or from injuries incurred while in care.
- Be no longer in need of medical care.
- Exhibit no signs of active disease.
- Have normal laboratory values, if tested (PCV, TS, BUN, etc.).
- Possess pelage or plumage that is adequate for that species to survive.
- Possess adequate vision to find/catch food and maneuver in a normal manner.
- Exhibit locomotive skills necessary for that species to survive.
- Demonstrate the fight or flight behavioral response.
- Demonstrate proper foraging behavior (self-feeding if raised in captivity).
- Demonstrate proper species behavior (e.g., not improperly imprinted).
- Be of correct age for independent survival.
- Be of correct weight for that sex, species, age, and season.
- Exhibit waterproof pelage/plumage sufficient for that species.

In addition to the above parameters for the condition of the animal, many other considerations must be made. Suitable habitat with an adequate food and water supply, appropriate weather, season, and time of day are necessary for a successful release. Releases must occur within the parameters of local, state, and federal regulations or laws. The proximity of busy roadways, the presence of natural or introduced predators (e.g., domestic cats), human developments, existing populations of that species, and long term food sources should always be factored into determining the suitability of a release site.

7.3 Minimum Standards for Euthanasia in Wildlife Rehabilitation

Definition

Euthanasia is defined as the induction of death with minimal pain, stress, or anxiety. Wildlife rehabilitators who direct the operation of a facility must make these decisions to euthanize animals, as well as perform or supervise the euthanasia procedures. They also must exhibit understanding and compassion for those who have been involved with the terminal case.

Criteria

While no ideal euthanasia agent exists, the procedure of choice should approach as closely as possible the following criteria:

- Produces rapid loss of consciousness and death
- Exhibits consistent and predictable action
- Is easily and safely administered by properly trained personnel
- Causes minimal psychological stress to the animal
- Causes minimal emotional effects to observers and participants
- Is not subject to abuse by humans
- Interrupts consciousness and reflexes simultaneously
- Is not a sanitation or environmental problem
- Results in no tissue changes that would affect a postmortem diagnosis
- Is economical and readily available

The method of euthanasia is only as humane as the knowledge and skill of the operator performing it. Individuals administering euthanasia should be trained in the process and have an understanding of how the particular method produces death in the animal. The safety of the operator should be given as much consideration as humaneness of the method.

7.3.1 Acceptable Euthanasia Methods

Below is a brief description of some methods of euthanasia recommended for use in wildlife. None of these methods should be used without proper training and, in the case of some of the regulated substances, without proper licensing. The *AVMA Guidelines on Euthanasia* (2011) and the AAZV 2006 *Guidelines for Euthanasia of Nondomestic Animals* provide additional information on methods of euthanasia for wildlife. Please note: The IWRC and the NWRA do not condone all of the methods in the *2000 Report of the AVMA Panel on Euthanasia* nor the *AVMA Guidelines on Euthanasia* (2007) as being appropriate for use in wildlife. Each wildlife rehabilitator is urged to seek and learn to use those methods which s/he feels are humane and within their legal and practical limits.

Physical Methods:

Cervical luxation/dislocation:
Causes death by severing the spinal cord and destroying ascending sensory (pain) pathways, resulting in depression of central nervous system (CNS), respiratory, and cardiac functions. Grasping the body of the animal and the base of the skull, the neck of the animal is hyper-extended. The neck is rotated in a down-and-away motion relative to the body position using the thumb and forefingers, separating the first cervical vertebra from the base of the skull and severing the spinal cord.
Advantages: Clean; safe to perform; moderately rapid; special equipment not required.
Disadvantages: Must be performed by skilled personnel. May be aesthetically objectionable to staff/volunteers/public. Should only be performed on small birds and mammals; animal may remain conscious for a brief period following dislocation (may convulse prior to death).

Decapitation:
Causes death by severing the spinal cord and destroying ascending sensory (pain) pathways, resulting in depression of CNS, respiratory, and cardiac functions.
Advantages: Moderately rapid; effective in reptiles, though movement may continue following decapitation; therefore, the brain of reptiles also must be pithed or otherwise destroyed to ensure that there is no residual brain activity.
Disadvantages: Must be performed by skilled personnel. May be aesthetically objectionable to staff/volunteers/public. Should only be performed on small animals; animal may remain conscious for a brief period following decapitation (may convulse prior to death).

Exsanguination:
Laceration of a major vessel (usually the jugular vein) results in rapid blood loss and decrease in blood pressure.
Advantages: Moderately rapid death; better if done on sedated, stunned, or anesthetized animals.
Disadvantages: May cause anxiety and pain in a conscious animal; requires skill and training; may be aesthetically unappealing.

Gunshot to the head:
Causes immediate unconsciousness by direct and rapid destruction of brain tissue when positioned properly.
Advantages: Rapid; can be used on most species.
Disadvantages: Must be performed by skilled personnel. Requires special equipment and may require firearm permit. May be aesthetically objectionable to staff/volunteers/public. Potential for human injury. Cannot be used for animals suspected of rabies unless a portion of the brain is left intact for lab testing, and care should be taken if using in rabies vector species to avoid accidental exposure to rabies-infected brain tissues via aerosolized particles. Improperly positioned shot may delay death.

Penetrating captive bolt:
Causes immediate unconsciousness by direct and rapid destruction of brain tissue when positioned properly against the skull and fired. This is one of the few options for euthanizing large ruminants or carnivores; also has been used on small ruminants.
Advantages: Rapid.
Disadvantages: Must be performed by skilled personnel. Requires special equipment and may require permit. May be aesthetically objectionable to staff/volunteers/public. Must be done at close range (nearly direct contact to the animal's skull) and the animal must be properly restrained or sedated to insure accuracy. Improperly positioned shot may delay death.

Adjunct Physical Methods (should not be used as sole method):

Pithing:
Causes direct destruction of brain and spinal cord as a needle or probe is inserted into the base of the skull.
Advantages: Rapid; one of the few methods effective in many reptiles.
Disadvantages: Must be done on an unconscious animal; requires skill and training; may be aesthetically unappealing.

Stunning (blunt force trauma):
Striking of the skull, resulting in unconsciousness of the animal.
Advantages: Rapid unconsciousness.
Disadvantages: Not a sole method of euthanasia—usually followed by exsanguination; requires skill to be done properly; may be aesthetically unappealing; should not be used if the brain must be examined (as with suspected rabies cases).

Inhalation Agents:

Care should be taken when using chambers to contain animals for euthanasia because overcrowding or mixing of species can cause severe apprehension and psychological stress prior to death.

Halothane, isoflurane, enflurane, sevoflurane and methoxyflurane:
Cause direct depression of CNS; should be done in a chamber in a well-ventilated area to reduce human exposure.
Advantages: Useful when venipuncture is difficult as with small animals such as birds, bats, rodents, and small carnivores; some of these agents are nonflammable and nonexplosive under ordinary conditions; generally aesthetic; causes very little change that interferes with necropsy results.
Disadvantages: Some agents can be injurious to personnel and must be used in well-ventilated areas or with gas-scavenging devices; very young, old, and/or respiratory impaired animals may be resistant to the effects and struggle for a period of time; diving birds and mammals may require a considerable length of time to reach respiratory arrest; some of these agents may be flammable or explosive under certain conditions.

Carbon dioxide (CO_2):
Useful for small animals in chambers. The animal is placed into the chamber prior to the addition of the carbon dioxide; once the animal is in the chamber, CO_2 is added to the chamber, sinks to the bottom and displaces the ambient air. Death is caused by direct depression of CNS, respiratory, and cardiac functions. Concentrated CO_2 gas is noxious and irritating, and can cause a conscious animal to become distressed if placed into a chamber already filled with CO_2. Dilute CO_2 (mixed with oxygen) is not recommended either, as this mixture has been shown to actually prolong the time of death as the ambient air is displaced at a much slower rate. If dry ice is used as a source of carbon dioxide, it should not come in contact with the animal.
Advantages: Easily available in compressed cylinders or as "dry ice"; inexpensive and safe to the human handler.
Disadvantages: Because it is heavier than air, incomplete filling of the chamber can permit a climbing animal to avoid a lethal dose. This method should not be used for animals with severely depressed respiratory rates (e.g., animals in hibernation, or turtles). Irritating to the mucous membranes. May not be effective with bats and newborn animals, as they have a very high tolerance for carbon dioxide. Beaver and other diving mammals and birds may hold their breath for extended periods of time therefore requiring longer time for the carbon dioxide to take effect.

Carbon monoxide:
Useful for small animals in chambers. Causes death by irreversibly binding with hemoglobin in the red blood cells.
Advantages: Easily available in compressed cylinders; rapid.
Disadvantages: Very hazardous to human health; this odorless, tasteless gas may be lethal in humans at as little as 0.4% concentration.

Ether and Chloroform:
Cause direct depression of CNS. Usually administered in a closed chamber within a well-ventilated room.
Advantages: Moderately rapid; inexpensive; most effective when used on small animals.
Disadvantages: Ether is explosive and can be irritating to the animal; chloroform is a known liver toxin and carcinogen; potential human health hazard if used in poorly ventilated area. Materials saturated with these substances must be handled carefully and disposed of properly to prevent harm to humans or animals that might come in contact with them.

Adjunct Inhalant Agents (should not be used as sole method):

Nitrous oxide:
Nitrous oxide alone is inadequate, but when used as a carrier gas, it speeds up the uptake of other volatile gases (halothane, isoflurane, enflurane, and methoxyflurane).

Non-inhalant pharmacologic agents:

Barbiturates:
(Pentobarbital) Intravenous or intra-cardiac injection results in direct depression of CNS, respiratory, and cardiac functions. Intra-abdominal injection may be acceptable in mammals when a vein is not accessible. Intramuscular injection will result in extensive tissue necrosis and pain.
Advantages: Rapid and smooth induction of unconsciousness; usually aesthetically acceptable to staff/volunteers/public.
Disadvantages: Intravenous administration is necessary for best results; requires Drug Enforcement Administration registration, record keeping, and special storage conditions. These drugs are subject to abuse by humans. They do not cause analgesia, and low doses may actually produce a hyperesthetic effect (i.e., the animal may actually become more sensitive to stimuli). High potential for secondary poisonings if carcasses are not disposed of properly.

T-61:
(Embutramide, mebozonium iodide, and tetracaine hydrochloride) Combination of a local anaesthetic, a strong hypnotic, and a paralytic agent. Slow intravenous or intra-cardiac injection results in loss of consciousness, direct depression of respiratory functions including paralysis of respiratory muscles, and circulatory collapse.
Advantages: Rapid and smooth induction of respiratory arrest and death; extremely fast and smooth-acting in birds; not a controlled drug; usually aesthetically acceptable to staff/ volunteers/public.
Disadvantages: Slow intravenous administration is necessary for best results; some mammals may vocalize or exhibit muscle contraction upon injection; requires record keeping, and special storage conditions due to potential for abuse by humans; not available in the United States. Potential for secondary poisonings if carcasses are not disposed of properly.

Preanesthetics:
(Ketamine, Xylazine, and others) can be given by intramuscular injection to both mammals and birds to facilitate euthanasia by another method. These drugs should not be used as sole euthanasia agents.

7.3.2 Unacceptable Euthanasia Methods

Many techniques have been used to provide death to wild animals, but many of these are also considered inhumane (therefore not true euthanasia) or extremely dangerous, and are not condoned under these *Minimum Standards for Wildlife Rehabilitation*. Methods which are **not** approved for use in wildlife are:

Acetone

Air embolism

Cyanide

Drowning

Electrocution

Engine starting fluid (10-12% ether, remainder petroleum distillates)

Freezing

Kill traps

Neuromuscular blocking agents used <u>alone</u> (succinylcholine, potassium chloride, magnesium sulfate); may be acceptable if used in combination with a sedative

Nitrogen or argon gas

Nitrous oxide used <u>alone</u>

Overdose of any non-euthanasia drug (e.g., aspirin, other NSAIDs, or antibiotics)

Strychnine

Thoracic compression

7.3.3 Disposal of Carcasses and Animal Waste Products

Animals that have been euthanized by chemical injection may contain enough drug to cause secondary poisonings if their carcases are scavanged. Such carcasses should be disposed of by incineration rather than landfill, and should NEVER be fed to other wildlife. Similarly, cloths, rags, or other materials used to apply substances such as chloroform and ether also may pose a threat to humans or wildlife if they are not disposed of properly. Proper methods for disposal of animal carcasses and waste products should be followed as described in section 2.3.5.

7.3.4 Disposal of Euthanasia Equipment and Chemicals

Single-use medical supplies used for performing euthanasia (syringes, needles, scalpels) should be disposed of properly. Medical sharps should be placed in a well-labeled container, and should be incinerated or taken to a local veterinary or human hospital for disposal. Syringes that might contain residues of drugs used for euthanasia also should be disposed of according to local /regional requirements for the disposal of medical waste; these syringes should NOT be autoclaved or reused for other purposes.

Empty vials or other containers previously containing euthanasia chemicals also should be disposed of according to local/regional requirements for the disposal of medical waste (usually incineration).

Appendix A – Forms

Forms 1-3: Facility Review

The information and questions contained in these three forms are a means for both rehabilitation facilities (**Form 1**) and individual rehabilitators (**Form 2**) to do a self-evaluation or self-review. The purpose is to provide wildlife care-givers suggestions to save time (for example, keeping reference materials at the phone), to ensure wildlife receives appropriate housing and medical treatment (exam area, caging, veterinary, and diagnostic), and to protect both wildlife and humans from disease and contamination (food preparation, disinfecting, housekeeping). Not all items contained in the forms will apply to everyone; the forms are meant to provide an easy reference to be sure important considerations are not overlooked, especially when changes occur such as facility growth or unexpected species or numbers are admitted. Above all, the rehabilitator needs to first abide by all local or regional codes that may apply (e.g., if radiograph equipment is on site, proper licensing and registration for that equipment must be obtained and maintained according to local regulations).

Form 3 is a checklist intended to be used in conjunction with the *Minimum Standards for Wildlife Rehabilitation* to help wildlife care-givers ensure that wildlife receives appropriate housing and medical treatment, and to protect both wildlife and humans from disease and contamination. This form also may be helpful to state, provincial, and federal agency personnel inspecting facilities.

Forms 4A-C: Sample Admission Forms

These forms are examples of admission forms used to gather information from the individual(s) presenting wildlife to the rehabilitator. These forms were chosen to represent a variety of possible formats the rehabilitator can use: the first is a paper form used for birds, the second is an electronic form used for all species, and the third is a paper form designed specifically for use with turtles. Each facility/rehabilitator is encouraged to design record-keeping methods that work well for their own needs and gather the information needed for use within the facility and in creating state, federal, and/or provincial reports.

Forms 5A-C: Sample Physical Examination Forms

These forms are examples of physical examination forms for birds, mammals, and turtles, respectively. Each facility/rehabilitator is encouraged to design record-keeping methods that work well for their own needs; these forms simply illustrate the types of information to be collected, and formats that have worked successfully for others.

Form 6: Data Form for Suspect Poisoning Cases

Form 7: Sample Questionnaire for Rabies Suspects

Appendix A – Form 1: Facility Review—Institutional Facilities

I. RECEIVING AREA

    A. Public Information

        1. Are there written policies or procedures for staff and volunteers dealing with wildlife problems?

        2. Does the organization have information available to the public on the services it provides for wildlife?

    B. Procedures: Does the organization have operational policies available to staff members and volunteers (e.g., operations manual, rules derived from Board decisions, or training materials)?

    C. Records   (Section 1.3)

        1. Is there a medical record for each animal that has a medical problem?

        2. Do animals without medical problems have records (e.g., orphans)?

        3. Are the records legible?

        4. Are records adequately completed (i.e., can the progress of the animal be followed by reviewing the record)?

        5. Is there a system to identify each animal to its record?

    D. Facilities

        1. Is the reception area neat and presentable?

        2. Is it organized so that resident patients are not subject to stress during the intake of new animals?

    E. Telephone Services: For those providing help, assistance ,and directions to the public, are protocols established to provide assistance in the following areas:

        1. Humanely preventing or reducing wildlife problems, conflict situations, and injury?

        2. Determining if animals in fact need to be rescued?

        3. Providing strategies and techniques to give opportunities for mother animals to retrieve temporarily displaced young or to re-nest?

        4. Suggesting safe capture, restraint, and transport techniques to minimize risk of injury to animals and to humans?

II. INTAKE/EXAM AREA (Section 1.2 and Table 1)

    A. Is the area clean?

    B. Is the area set up so that animals can be examined safely?

    C. Are first-aid supplies available?

    D. Are there scales available to weigh animals as part of intake and assessment?

    E. Are animals awaiting exam/treatment provided a warm, quiet, and dark place?

F. Are facilities arranged and/or constructed to minimize stress on the animals?

G. Are the sound and activity levels minimized to reduce stress on the animal?

H. Are capture and handling equipment easily accessible and in good working order? Are they used safely?

I. Are capture, handling, and restraint procedures safe for animals and humans?

J. Are the people handling wildlife trained in safe handling techniques?

III. FACILITIES FOR INTENSIVE NURSING CARE

☐ Available at a veterinary facility   ☐ Available on-site

A. Are the following available for use when necessary?

☐ Incubators   ☐ Heat sources (lamps, pads)

B. Is the area clean?

C. Is it a low-traffic area?

IV. SURGERY

☐ Available at veterinary clinic/hospital   ☐ Available on-site

A. Is the area aseptic?

B. Is there resuscitative equipment available?

C. Is there a pre-surgical prep area?

D. Is the surgical equipment in good working order?

V. RADIOLOGY SERVICES

☐ Available at veterinary clinic/hospital   ☐ Available on-site

A. Do individuals taking radiographs have dosimetry badges to monitor exposure?

B. Is the radiation equipment inspected annually (or per state requirements)?

VI. INITIAL CARE FACILITIES (Sections 3.2.1 and 3.4)

A. Do the cages meet caging standards for the species handled?

B. Are they constructed so that they can be cleaned and disinfected (e.g., stainless steel, fiberglass, sealed wood, coated port-a-pets)?

C. Are the cages cleaned regularly (as appropriate for the species and cage type)?

D. Is the area adequately ventilated in an appropriate manner?

E. Is there adequate lighting (full-spectrum light at the appropriate hours)?

F. Are isolation facilities available (on-site, at a veterinary clinic, elsewhere)?

G. Is the area away from the main flow of human activity?

H. Is there access to the area by domestic pets?

VII. PRIMARY EXERCISE CAGING (Sections 3.2.2, 3.2.3 and 3.5)

    A. Do they meet caging standards for the species being handled?

    B. Are they cleanable?

    C. Is there a regular cleaning schedule?

    D. Are they safe to the handlers and animals being held (e.g., no loose or sharp wires or nails, double doors, etc.)?

    E. Are they secure (e.g., locking, sturdy, safe from predators)?

VIII. PHARMACY

    A. Is the area clean and organized?

    B. Are needed medications on hand? Are other medications available by prescription or through sponsoring organizations?

    C. Are controlled drugs (schedules II, III, IV) kept in locked, secure location?

    D. Is there a log for controlled drugs?

    E. Are antibiotics, parasiticides, vaccines, etc., available either in the pharmacy or on a prescription basis?

    F. Are emergency medications available?

IX. DISINFECTING (Section 2.4)

    A. Is there a standard procedure and schedule for cleaning and disinfecting cages, feeding utensils, syringes, food storage containers, and food, water, and bathing bowls?

    B. Are cleaning and disinfecting supplies available and stored properly?
        1. Is human protective gear (gloves, masks, goggles) available?
        2. Are instructions on the proper use of disinfectants displayed?

    C. Is there a designated area for storage, cleaning, and disinfecting of dirty items?

    D. Is there a designated area for storage of clean and disinfected items?

X. PATHOLOGY SERVICES (Section 2.3.5)

☐ Available on-site   ☐ Available through veterinarian   ☐ Commercial account

Can the following services be provided to wildlife when necessary?

    A. Hematology (PCV, Diff., Hb, WBC, Clot Time, ESR, Serum Chemistries)?

    B. Parasitology?

    C. Microbiology?

    D. Necropsy Services?
        If done in shelter:
        1. Are separate instruments used for tissue gathering and necropsy?
        2. Are dead animals disposed of in accordance with applicable ordinances or regulations?

XI. FOOD PREPARATION & STORAGE

    A. Is the area clean, orderly?

    B. Are adequate foodstuffs and supplies available?

    C. Are foodstuffs (chicks, rats, fish) stored separately from dead (rehabilitation) animals?

    D. Are perishable foodstuffs dated (open formula)?

XII. HOUSEKEEPING & MAINTENANCE (Section 2.4)

    A. Is there a reasonable schedule for:

        1. Daily cleaning?

        2. Weekly cleaning?

        3. Seasonal cleaning?

    B. Is there a continuing program for repair and upkeep of the facility?

XIII. LIBRARY

    A. Is there a continuing program for acquisition of pertinent publications on wildlife rehabilitation?

    B. Are manuals/books available on providing humane solutions to human/wildlife conflicts?

    C. Are publications available that describe each species and its natural history?

XIV. SAFETY

    A. Is there a fire alarm?

    B. Is there a fire extinguisher(s)?

    C. Are eating, drinking, smoking, etc., restricted to designated areas?

    D. Is there a first-aid kit available for staff/volunteers?

    E. Are material data safety sheets (MSDSs) readily available/easily accessible for those chemicals used at the facility (disinfectants, cleansers, certain drugs, etc.)?

XV. ORGANIZATIONAL STANDARDS

    A. Does the individual or organization comply with local ordinances and have current state/provincial/federal permits for the work being done?

    B. Is there a grievance policy for staff/volunteers?

    C. Is there a training policy for staff/volunteers?

    D. Are there continuing training opportunities for staff (paid and volunteer) who have completed basic skills training (staff training sessions, IWRC and NWRA programs, etc.)?

    E. Is there a liability insurance policy for volunteers to protect the facility and/or organization?

F. Is there a workers compensation policy for employees?

G. What after-hours services are available for emergency cases (on-call person, emergency veterinary clinic services, etc.)?

H. Are there written policies to instruct the volunteers regarding rules of the organization as they relate to animal care, reporting procedures, rules on conduct?

XVI. CONTINUING EDUCATION

A. Is pertinent information collected on wildlife rehabilitation?

B. Does the permittee's organization collect such information and share it with other members?

C. Does the permittee and/or others in the organization attend continuing education classes or conferences on wildlife rehabilitation?

Appendix A – Form 2: Facility Review—Out-of-Shelter Facilities

I. INITIAL CARE FACILITIES:

- A. Do the cages meet caging standards for the species handled?
- B. Are they constructed so that they can be cleaned and disinfected (i.e., stainless steel, fiberglass, sealed wood, coated port-a-pets)?
- C. Are isolation facilities available (on-site, at a veterinary clinic, elsewhere)?
- D. Are the cages cleaned daily?
- E. Is the area ventilated?
- F. Does the area have adequate lighting?
- G. Is the area away from the main flow of family life?
- H. Is access to the area by family pets restricted?

II. OUTDOOR/UNLIMITED EXERCISE CAGING:

- A. Do the enclosures meet caging standards for the species being handled?
- B. Are they cleanable?
- C. Is there a regular cleaning schedule?
- D. Are they secure (i.e., locking, sturdy)?
- E. Are they safe to the handlers and animals being held (i.e., loose or sharp wire, nails, double doors)?

III. MEDICATIONS:

- A. Are needed medications on hand?
- B. Are other medications available by prescription or through sponsoring organizations?

IV. VETERINARY SERVICES:

- A. Are veterinary services provided for the animals being held?
- B. Do those services include, when necessary, the following:
  1. Examination?
  2. Diagnostic Services?
  3. Radiology?
  4. Clinical Pathology?
  5. Necropsy Services?
  6. Surgery?

V. RECORDS:

- A. Are records kept for each animal under care?
- B. Are they legible?
- C. Are they adequately completed (can the progress of the animal be followed by reviewing the record)?
- D. Is there a system to identify each animal to its record?

VI. FACILITIES FOR INTENSIVE NURSING CARE:

☐ Available at a veterinary facility   ☐ Provided by permittee?

A. Are the following available for use when necessary?

☐ Incubators   ☐ Heat sources (lamps, pads)   ☐ Other?

B. Is the area clean, orderly?

C. Is it a low-traffic area?

VII. FOOD PREPARATION & STORAGE:

A. Are Is the area clean, orderly?

B. Are adequate foodstuffs and supplies available?

C. Are dead animals stored so that family food will not be contaminated?

D. Are perishable foodstuffs dated (i.e., open formula)?

VIII. HOUSEKEEPING & MAINTENANCE:

A. Is there a reasonable schedule for:
   1. Daily cleaning?
   2. Weekly cleaning?
   3. Seasonal cleaning?

B. Is there a continuing program for repair and upkeep of cages and equipment?

IX. CONTINUING EDUCATION:

A. Do you collect pertinent information on wildlife rehabilitation?

B. Does the permittee collect such information and share it with volunteers and others involved?

C. Do you attend continuing education classes or conferences on wildlife rehabilitation?

X. ORGANIZATIONAL STANDARDS (For permittees who work under an out-of-shelter permit issued to an organization):

A. Does either the permittee or organization have current state/provincial/federal permits
for the animals under care?

B. Individual rehabilitators without an organization must also show proof of valid authorization from the state/provincial/federal government.

C. Is there a training policy that provides for initial training for new recruits?

D. Is there a liability insurance policy for volunteers to protect the organization?

E. What after-hours services are available for emergency cases (this can be offered by on-call volunteers, veterinary clinic, etc.)?

F. Are there written policies to instruct the volunteers regarding rules of the organization as they relate to animal care, reporting procedures, rules on conduct?

Appendix A – Form 3: Checklist for facilitating the use of the MSWR

This checklist is intended to be used in conjunction with the *Minimum Standards for Wildlife Rehabilitation* to help wildlife care-givers ensure that wildlife receives appropriate housing and medical treatment, and to protect both wildlife and humans from disease and contamination. *The italicized items are intended to help state, provincial, and federal agency personnel inspecting facilities. Section numbers refer to the section of* Minimum Standards *that has information about this topic.*

Background

Organization/Rehabilitator: _____ Date:_____

Fed Rehabilitation PRT #_____ Exp. Date_____

State Rehabilitation PRT #_____ Exp. Date_____

Fed Special Purpose Possession/Education permit_____ Exp. Date_____

State Education PRT#_____ Exp. Date_____

Species rehabilitated: birds   mammals   reptiles   amphibians

Name of Permit holder:_____

Number of paid staff:_____ # volunteers on site:_____

Number of individuals rehabilitating off-site under authorization of above permits _____

Names:_____

Addresses:_____

(use additional sheet if necessary)

Are Outreach/Education programs conducted on-site?   Y/N   off-site?   Y/N

Is veterinary care available on-site?   Y/N   off-site?   Y/N

Name of vet(s) _____ Phone # _____

_____ Phone # _____

Do you network or cooperate with other permitted rehabilitators?   Y/N

In what capacity do you network with other rehabilitators? (i.e., flight cages, etc.)

(use additional sheet if necessary) _____

_____

Who are the rehabilitators you network with? (use additional sheet if necessary)

_____

_____

Have you given written permission to federal and/or state agencies allowing them to refer calls concerning sick or injured wild animals to you?   Y/N

<u>*Y*</u> <u>*N*</u> *(Please check the appropriate box for each item in the Checklist)*

TELEPHONE SERVICES

For those providing help, assistance, and directions to the public, are protocols established to provide assistance in the following areas:

☐ ☐ *Humanely preventing or reducing wildlife problems, conflict situations, and injury; provide advice if species not accepted?*

☐ ☐ *Determining if animals in fact need to be rescued?*

☐ ☐ *Providing strategies and techniques to give opportunities for mother animals to retrieve temporarily displaced young or to re-nest?*

☐ ☐ *Suggesting safe capture, restraint, and transport techniques to minimize risk of injury to animals and to humans?*

RECEPTION OR INTAKE AREA

☐ ☐ *Is the reception area neat and presentable?*

☐ ☐ *Are there established procedures for receiving animals?*

☐ ☐ *Is educational material available for the public?*

☐ ☐ *Is natural history material available for responding to inquiries?*

☐ ☐ *Are brochures for the center/organization available?*

TRAINING & EDUCATION (Section 2.3)

Are there written policies and/or procedures for staff and volunteers regarding:

☐ ☐ *Zoonotic diseases and proper animal handling protocols?*

☐ ☐ *The use of safety equipment (goggles, gloves, nets, etc.)*

☐ ☐ *The use of disposable gloves and masks?* ☐ ☐ *Are they readily available?*

☐ ☐ *The first aid kit; and is a kit available?*

☐ ☐ *Insurance for staff and/or volunteers?*

☐ ☐ *Are there operational policies available to staff members and volunteers (e.g., operations manual, rules derived from Board decisions, or training materials)?*

☐ ☐ *Is continuing education available to staff/permittees?*

☐ ☐ Publications, conferences, networking opportunities

☐ ☐ Method to update staff and volunteers of new procedures in the field

☐ ☐ Does the permittee and/or others in the organization attend continuing education classes or conferences on wildlife rehabilitation?

☐ ☐ Is there a resource library?

☐ ☐ Is there a program for acquisition of pertinent publications on rehabilitation?

☐ ☐ Is material available on humane solutions to human/wildlife conflicts?

☐ ☐ Are publications available that describe each species and its natural history?

☐ ☐ *Is information available to educate the public on wildlife issues?*

Minimum Standards for Wildlife Rehabilitation, 4th edition, 2012, NWRA & IWRC

Y N *(Please check the appropriate box for each item in the Checklist)*

SAFETY

☐ ☐ Is there a fire alarm?

☐ ☐ Is there a fire extinguisher(s)?

☐ ☐ *Are eating, drinking, smoking, etc., restricted to designated areas?*

☐ ☐ *Is there a first-aid kit available for staff/volunteers?*

☐ ☐ Are material data safety sheets (MSDSs) readily available/easily accessible for those chemicals used at the facility (disinfectants, cleansers, certain drugs, etc.)?

☐ ☐ Are capture and handling equipment easily accessible and in good working order?

☐ ☐ Are capture, handling, and restraint procedures safe for animals and humans?

☐ ☐ Are the people handling wildlife trained in safe handling techniques?

RECORDS (Section 1.3)

☐ ☐ *Is there a medical record for each animal?*

☐ ☐ *Are records organized and maintained with appropriate information (i.e., can the progress of the animal be followed by reviewing the record)?*

☐ ☐ *Is there a system to identify each animal to its record and is there a record keeping daily log system? (leg tags, ear tags, cage numbers, etc.)*

☐ ☐ *Is a computerized database maintained?*

☐ ☐ *Are copies of annual reports readily available?*

INTAKE/EXAM AREA (Section 1.2 and Table 1)

☐ ☐ *Is the area clean?*

☐ ☐ Is the area quiet?

☐ ☐ *Is the area set up so animals can be examined safely, securely, and out of public view?*

☐ ☐ *Are first-aid supplies available?*

☐ ☐ Are the appropriate sized scales available?

☐ ☐ Are animals awaiting exam/treatment provided a warm, quiet, and dark place?

☐ ☐ Are facilities arranged or organized to minimize stress on the animals?

☐ ☐ Is the appropriate equipment available (incubators, exam light, stethoscope, etc.)?

☐ ☐ *Are the sound and activity levels minimized to reduce stress on the animal?*

_**Y N**_ *(Please check the appropriate box for each item in the Checklist)*

SURGERY

☐ ☐ *Available at veterinary clinic/hospital?*

☐ ☐ *Available on-site? If yes:*

☐ ☐ Is the area aseptic?

☐ ☐ Is there resuscitative equipment available?

☐ ☐ Is there a pre-surgical prep area?

☐ ☐ Is the surgical equipment in good working order?

☐ ☐ Is the anesthetic equipment maintained?

☐ ☐ If gas anesthesia is used, is the area well ventilated?

RADIOLOGY SERVICES

☐ ☐ *Available at veterinary clinic/hospital?*

☐ ☐ *Available on-site? If yes:*

☐ ☐ Does each individual taking radiographs have a dosimetry badge to monitor exposure?

☐ ☐ Is the radiation equipment inspected annually (or per state requirements)?

PHARMACY/MEDICATIONS

☐ ☐ *Are needed medications on hand? Are other medications available by prescription or through sponsoring organizations?*

☐ ☐ *If controlled drugs (schedules II, III, IV) are kept on site, are they in a locked, secure location?*

☐ ☐ *Is there a log for controlled drugs?*

☐ ☐ Are antibiotics, parasiticides, vaccines, etc., available either on-site or on a prescription basis?

☐ ☐ Are appropriate formularies or protocols available to provide drug dosages?

PATHOLOGY SERVICES (Section 2.3.5)

Can pathology services be provided to wildlife when necessary? (on- or off-site):

☐ ☐ Hematology (PCV, Diff., Hb, WBC, Clot Time, ESR, Serum Chemistries)?

☐ ☐ Parasitology?

☐ ☐ Microbiology?

☐ ☐ *Necropsy Services? If done on-site:*

☐ ☐ *are necropsies conducted in a well-ventilated area?*

☐ ☐ *are appropriate gloves and masks available?*

Y   N   *(Please check the appropriate box for each item in the Checklist)*

HOUSEKEEPING & MAINTENANCE (Sections 2.3 and 2.4)

Is there a reasonable schedule for:

☐ ☐ *Daily cleaning?*

☐ ☐ *Weekly cleaning?*

☐ ☐ *Seasonal cleaning?*

☐ ☐ *Is there a standard procedure and schedule for cleaning and disinfecting cages, feeding utensils, syringes, food storage containers, and food, water, and bathing bowls?*

☐ ☐ *Are cleaning and disinfecting supplies available and stored properly?*

☐ ☐ *Is human protective gear (gloves, masks, goggles) available?*

☐ ☐ *Are instructions on the proper use of disinfectants displayed?*

☐ ☐ *Is there a designated area for storage, cleaning, and disinfecting of dirty items?*

☐ ☐ *Is there a continuing program for repair and upkeep of the facility?*

FACILITIES FOR INTENSIVE NURSING CARE

☐ ☐ Available at veterinary clinic/hospital? If off-site, are animals housed away from domestic/other unsuitable animals?

☐ ☐ Available on-site?

CAGING: List number, size, and type of cages available on site (Use additional sheet). (Chapters 3,4,5, & 6)

INDOOR CAGING (Sections 3.2.1 and 3.4; Tables 3-7)

☐ ☐ Do the cages meet minimum sizes for the species handled?

☐ ☐ *Are they constructed so they can be cleaned and disinfected, with appropriate flooring (e.g., stainless steel, fiberglass, sealed wood, coated port-a-pets)?*

☐ ☐ *Can different species be adequately separated (e.g., predator/prey species)?*

☐ ☐ *Are the cages cleaned regularly (as appropriate for the species and cage type)?*

☐ ☐ *Is the area adequately ventilated in an appropriate manner?*

☐ ☐ *Is adequate lighting provided (full-spectrum light at the appropriate hours)?*

☐ ☐ *Do cages provide visual barriers or hiding areas for the animal?*

☐ ☐ *Are food and water presented in an appropriate manner for each species?*

☐ ☐ *Are isolation facilities available (on-site, at a veterinary clinic, elsewhere)?*

☐ ☐ *Is the area away from the main flow of human activity?*

☐ ☐ *Are facilities secure to protect wildlife from undue disturbance or harm from humans, wild animals, domestic animals, and/or pets?*

Y N *(Please check the appropriate box for each item in the Checklist)*

OUTDOOR CAGING (Section 3.2.3 and 3.5; Tables 3-7)

☐ ☐ Do the cages meet minimum sizes for the species being handled?

☐ ☐ *Are they cleaned and disinfected easily and constructed with appropriate flooring for species housed?*

☐ ☐ *Is there a regular cleaning schedule?*

☐ ☐ *Are they safe to the handlers and animals being held (e.g., no loose or sharp wires or nails, double doors, prevent escapes, etc.)?*

☐ ☐ *Are they secure to protect wildlife from undue disturbance or harm from humans, wild animals, domestic animals, and/or pets?*

☐ ☐ *Do the cages provide protection from the elements (wind, rain, snow, excess heat)?*

☐ ☐ *Are they appropriately distanced from cages of incompatible species or individuals?*

☐ ☐ *Do they provide visual barriers (shade cloth, hide boxes, etc.) to minimize stress?*

☐ ☐ *Do they have a double-entry system?*

☐ ☐ *Do they provide appropriate ventilation, sun, and shade?*

☐ ☐ *Do all cages have the appropriate perches?*

FOOD PREPARATION & STORAGE

☐ ☐ *Is there a separate storage area for animal food (separate from human food and separate from carcasses)?*

☐ ☐ *Is food labeled and in vermin-proof containers, and are feeding schedules posted with amount, time, and animal identification?*

☐ ☐ *Is the area clean, orderly?*

☐ ☐ Are adequate foodstuffs and supplies available?

☐ ☐ Are perishable foodstuffs dated (e.g., open formula)?

Y **N** *(Please check the appropriate box for each item in the Checklist)*

RELEASE (Section 7.2)

☐ ☐ *Are written release criteria and protocols available?*

☐ ☐ *Do animals receive a pre-release examination?*

☐ ☐ *Are soft-release techniques used?*

☐ ☐ *Are hard-release techniques used?*

☐ ☐ *Is any live-prey testing done prior to release?*

　　　　If yes, are written policies/procedures available to staff and volunteers?

☐ ☐ *Are foster species used, appropriate permit number _____?*

　　　　If yes, which species?_____

☐ ☐ *Are animals marked in any way (banded, tagged, etc.)?*

☐ ☐ *Is any post-release monitoring conducted?*

☐ ☐ *Are there any pre-release flight conditioning policies and procedures or equipment? (e.g., flight cages, creancing, cooperative work with a falconer)*

☐ ☐ *Are guidelines for suitable release sites available and do you work with wildlife agency personnel on site selection?*

EUTHANASIA (Section 7.3)

☐ ☐ *Is there a written policy on who makes the decision?*

☐ ☐ *Is there a list of methods of euthanasia used?*

☐ ☐ Are there written protocols guiding which animals should be euthanized?

CARCASS AND WASTE DISPOSAL (Section 2.3.5)

☐ ☐ *Is there appropriate storage for carcasses* and schedule *for disposal of carcasses?*

☐ ☐ *Are dead animals disposed of in accordance with applicable ordinances or regulations?*

Appendix A – Form 4A: Sample Patient Admission Form—Birds

PATIENT ADMISSION FORM

DATE ___/___/____   SPECIES _____   CASE #:_____-_____

Time _____   Admitted by _____   Transported by _____

PLEASE COMPLETE THE FOLLOWING INFORMATION TO THE BEST OF YOUR KNOWLEDGE:

Name (person who found bird) Mr. Mrs. Ms. _____

Address _____   City/State/Zip_____

Email Address _____   Phone (____)_____

Date/time you first saw bird(s)? _____   Date/time captured? _____

Where specifically was it found (in yard, by window, etc.)? _____

Address where found _____   City/State/Zip_____

County _____   Nearest Intersection _____

Did you feed the bird? _____   If yes, what and how? _____

What else did you do to help the bird? _____

Please circle any of the following that pertain to this bird and its capture:

Easy/hard to catch	Parents/nestmates dead	Hit by vehicle	Trapped/entangled
Can't stand/ fly	Attacked by cat/dog/bird	Found in/beside road	Fishing line/hook
Hopping on ground	Hit window	Oiled or sticky	Shot or bleeding
Nest destroyed	Found by window	Wet or cold	Exposed to chemical/toxin

Additional remarks:_____

Wild birds admitted to this facility become the sole responsibility of the organization.
We are licensed by the state and federal governments to provide care for wild animals.

YES! I support the work of this organization with my tax deductible gift of $ _____
If you are leaving a cash donation and would like to be acknowledged, please put it in one of the
envelopes provided and clearly print your name on it before placing it in the donation box

---

FOR OFFICE USE ONLY: Check if referral _____ or re-admission _____

Assumed Cause of Injury Attack by cat / dog / other   Contaminant/ Oiled   Dangerous site (describe)

Disease (FES/ pox / WNV / other)   Electrocution/burns   Entrapment (specify)   Fell from nest

Gunshot   Hit by vehicle   Human interference (describe)   Impact (specify)   Nest destroyed

Nutritional/ developmental   Orphaned   Toxin (botulism/ lead / other)   Undetermined (acute/chronic)

Other/ Comment_____

Types of Injury Primary Behavioral   Contaminant   Feather damage   Gen'l debilitation

Neurologic   Ophthalmic   Orthopedic   Parasites   Respiratory   Soft tissue   No appt injury

Other/Comment:_____

Secondary Behavioral   Contaminant   Feather damage   Gen'l debilitation   Neurologic

Ophthalmic   Orthopedic   Parasites   Respiratory   Soft tissue   Other/ Comment: _____

Disposition: Date _____Init_____**Final Cause of Injury**_____

DBA   Died   EOA   Euth   Rel   Rel/Rtn to Nest   Rel/placed   Transf **by** _____

Rel Location _____Band # _____-_____

Appendix A – Form 4B: Sample Patient Admission Form—Electronic

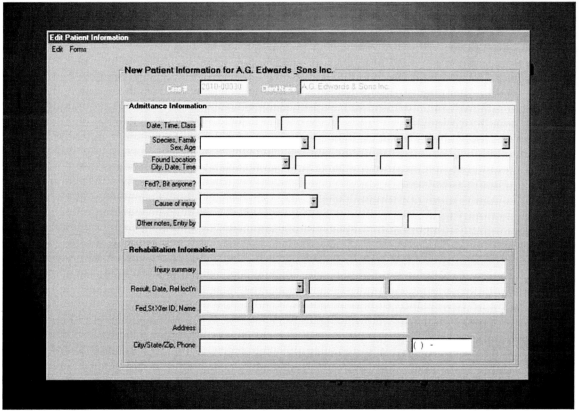

Electronic admission form - Primary Screen: Presenter's contact information

Electronic admission form - Secondary Screen: Patient history and disposition

Appendix A – Form 4C: Sample Patient Admission Form—Turtles

Case Number:

TURTLE ADMITTANCE RECORD – NATIVE SPECIES

Species:_____ Sex: **M F**   Age: **Adult Juvenile Hatchling**

Date:_____   email_____

Finder's Name:_____

Address: _____

_____

Phone: _____

Where turtle was found: Street: _____

Town: _____

County: _____

Length of time in finder's care: _____

Hit By Car ☐   Caught By Dog ☐   Fishhook ☐   Ear abscess ☐

Other: _____

_____

_____

Results:

DOA _____   Euthanized: _____

Died within 24 hours _____   Died: _____

Transferred: _____

Released: _____

Place of release: _____

Appendix A – Form 5A: Sample Patient Examination Form—Birds

PHYSICAL EXAM

DATE: ____/____/____ SPECIES: _____ CASE #: _____ - _____

TIME: _____ INITIALS: _____ WEIGHT: _____ TAG #: _____

BODY CONDITION: emaciated   underweight   normal   overweight   AGE/SEX: _____

HYDRATION: good   fair   poor   TEMP: _____

ATTITUDE: BAR   Remarks:_____

NARES: Clear   Remarks: _____

BEAK/MOUTH: WNL   Remarks: _____

RESPIRATION: WNL   Remarks: _____

CROP: full   empty   Remarks: _____

GI TRACT/ABDM: WNL   Remarks: _____

DROPPINGS: WNL   none   Remarks: _____

EYES: WNL Remarks: _____

EARS: WNL Remarks: _____

FEATHERS: WNL Remarks: _____

ECTO-PARASITES: none   Remarks: _____

SKIN: WNL Remarks: _____

FEET: WNL Remarks: _____

NERVOUS SYSTEM: WNL   Remarks: _____

_____

MUSCULOSKELETAL: WNL   Remarks: _____

_____

INJURIES/PROBLEMS (wounds, etc.): _____

_____

_____

_____

_____

On Entry:

D2.5LRS _____

abx _____

PO _____

Fecal _____

Other _____

PCV: _____%

BC: _____%

TS: _____g/dL

Initial Location

Please mark Cause of Injury and Type of Injury on Front of Form

INITIAL EXAM FORM

CASE # _____   INITIALS_____

SPECIES _____   ID _____

CAUSE OF INJURY:

ATTITUDE: NAFI/BAR*   ALERTLETHARGIC   UNCONCIOUS

TEMPERATURE: HYPOTHERMIC   HYPERTHERMIC

BODY CONDITION: OVERWEIGHT NORMAL   THIN EMACIATED

HYDRATION: GOOD   FAIR DEHYDRATED: _____% **WEIGHT:**_____

EYES: CLOSED BOTH L R NONREACTIVE BOTH L R LESIONS BOTH L R BLOOD BOTH L R

EARS: DISCHARGE   BLOOD   FLY EGGS   MAGGOTS

MOUTH: DRY   PALE   BLOOD   FLY EGGS   MAGGOTS

NOSE: DISCHARGE   BLOOD

RESPIRATION: RAPID SLOW LABORED   OPEN-MOUTH   APNEA

CARDIOVASCULAR:

GASTRO-INTESTINAL:

UROGENITAL:

NEURO: CNS SIGNS   HEAD TILT   NYSTAGMUS   SEIZURES

MUSCULAR/SKELETAL:

    LEGS: SOFT TISSUE DAMAGE: BOTH L R FRONT   REAR

                    FRACTURE: BOTH L R FEMUR   TIBIA   FIBULA   TARAUS   METATARSUS

                            BOTH L R HUMERUS RADIUS ULNA CARPUS METACARPUS

    FEET: BOTH L R FRONT REAR

    TOES: CURLED   INJURED   MISSING   FRACTURE

SKIN: PUNCTURE CUTS ABRASIONS BRUISED FLY EGGS   MAGGOTS   LOCATION_____

FUR: DIRTY   BLOODY   MISSING   FLEAS/PARASITES

FECES: LOOSE   BLOOD   BLACK   GREEN   NONE

COMMENTS:

*NO APPARENT FRACTURES OR INJURIES / BRIGHT ALERT and RESPONSIVE

TURTLE EXAMINATION FORM

Condition: alert   lethargic   unconscious

Hydration: normal   dehydrated (slight / moderate / severe)

Respiration: normal   open mouth   labored   noise   other _____

Neurological: normal   head tilt   circling   other_____

Head:	normal	trauma	fracture	blood	fly eggs	maggots
skull						
upper beak						
lower beak						

Notes:

Mouth: normal   blood   discharge   fly eggs   maggots

Glottis: clear   debris   blood   mucous

Color: normal   pale   red   other

Notes:

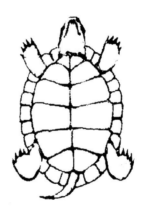
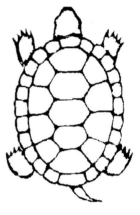

Ears: normal   trauma   swelling
discharge   blood   fly eggs   maggots

Notes:

Eyes: normal   clear   open   closed
trauma   swelling   sunken
discharge   blood   fly eggs   maggots

Notes:

Nose: normal   discharge   blood   trauma
fracture   depigmentation   erosion

Notes:

Shell:	normal	trauma	fracture	fly eggs	maggots	blood	discharge	odor	discoloration
Carapace									
Plastron									
Bridge									

Notes:

	normal	trauma	fracture	fly eggs	maggots	missing
Legs:						
Feet:						
Toes:						

Notes:

Skin: normal   dry/flaky   discoloration   punctures   cuts   abrasions   fly eggs   maggots

Cloaca: normal   trauma   swelling   discharge   fly eggs   maggots

Weight at admittance:

Observations:

Appendix A – Form 6: Data Form for Suspect Poisoning Cases

FISH AND WILDLIFE PESTICIDE POISONING INCIDENT FORM   Date: _____

1. Contact Name: _____

    Address/Telephone No.: _____

2. Date(s) of Incident: _____ Observation: _____

3. Pesticide(s) Suspected: _____

4. Analysis: (Attach laboratory reports or summarize below)
    a. Residue analysis:
    b. Enzyme analysis:
    c. Necropsy:

5. Location:

6. Land Use:

7. Meteorlogical Conditions:

8: Organisms Involved:

Species	**Number**	**Age/Size**	**Condition/Comments/Analysis Results**
_____	_____	_____	_____
_____	_____	_____	_____
_____	_____	_____	_____
_____	_____	_____	_____
_____	_____	_____	_____
_____	_____	_____	_____

9. Other Information:
    a. Circumstantial Evidence:
    b. Proximity to Pesticide Use:
    c. Pesticide Use Rate:
    d. Crop, acreage treated, any irrigation?
    e. Evidence of misapplication?

10. Other Comments: _____
    _____
    _____

Send To:

        CANDACE BRASSARD
        MAIL CODE 7507C
        US EPA
        WASHINGTON, DC 20460
        TELEPHONE: (703) 305-6598

HOW TO FILL OUT FORM (Please provide as much information as possible)

1. Name, title, address, and telephone number of individual to contact for further information. If observer is different than contact, provide name and address under other comments.

2. Date of observation and estimated date(s) of incident if different than date of observation.

3. Provide names (common or chemical) and fomulations of suspected pesticides.

4. Provide results of any analysis conducted during the investigation. Provide laboratory reports if possible. Some of this information may be easier to include below under the category of "Organisms Involved".
   a. Measured residues in carcass (species and concentration) or in food items or soil (identify type and location relative to affected animals);
   b. Acetylcholinesterase analysis or other enzyme analysis (species, measured values and values of controls or references); and
   c. Provide information from any other analysis or examination of carcasses.

5. Area and Location: City, Town, County, State, etc. If possible, identify location of incident by landmarks (e.g. roads, waterways, distance and direction from intersection, etc.). Any information on the area involved (e.g. acres, meters^2, miles^2, river miles, etc.) where effected animals were found. Describe topography and other land features as they may relate to pesticide movement or locating organisms.

6. Land use of area around incident. Indicate if urban or suburban, agricultural (specify), woods, wetlands (specify type), or other specific information about habitat. Especially note thickness of vegetation where organisms were located as this relates to how easily other carcasses could be found.

7. Meteorological conditions that could relate to incident, especially rainfall and wind at time incident occurred. Also note conditions that may have effected locating affected organisms. That is, under some weather conditions it is more difficult to find carcasses.

8. Organisms Involved: List species and provide number of each. Under age/size, indicate if organisms were young or adult. If there were mixed sizes, use a separate line for each size category or just indicate "mixed". Provide length or weight of fish. Under conditions, indicate if organisms were emaciated, healthy, injured, weakened, sick, or dead; probably exposed but no apparent effects; collected, died after collection, rehabilitated, released, frozen, analyzed, etc. Also, if one incident involved mortalities or affects on separate dates, indicate under "comments" the date of observation or occurrence for each group of organisms.

9. Discuss other factors, relating to pesticides such as:
   a. Circumstantial evidence suggesting pesticides may have caused the incident, e.g., dead birds in field where pesticide was used and pesticide has history of killing birds, etc.;
   b. Provide any available information on pesticide use;
   c. How close were pesticides used? (immediate area or distance in meters);
   d. Application rates, methods (aerial, ground) equipment, formulation; and,
   e. Crop, acreage treated, any irrigation.

10. Provide any other pertinent information either not included above, or as continuations from above. Use additional paper if necessary.

NOTE: This form may be copied as needed; instructions should be made available with the form. All participation is voluntary. Information, once provided to EPA, may be made available to the public.

Appendix A – Form 7: Sample Questionnaire for Rabies Suspect Specimens

QUESTIONNAIRE FOR RABIES SUSPECT SPECIMENS

DATE SUBMITTED _____

SENDER/SUBMITTER	OWNER OR GAME COMMISSION
_____	_____
_____	_____
_____	_____
Phone (____) ____ - _____	Phone (____) ____ - _____

KIND OF ANIMAL TO BE TESTED_____ PET _____ STRAY_____ WILDLIFE_____

BREED _____ SEX_____ AGE_____

NEAREST MAILING ADDRESS TO LOCATION WHERE INCIDENT OCCURRED

STREET_____ TOWN_____ ZIP CODE_____

COUNTY_____ TOWNSHIP_____ CITY_____ BORO_____

WAS ANY PERSON BITTEN/EXPOSED OR SCRATCHED?   Yes _____   No _____   Unknown _____

If so, please describe the incident_____

WAS ANY ANIMAL BITTEN OR SCRATCHED?   Yes_____   No _____   Unknown _____

Was the bitten animal vaccinated against rabies? If YES, When_____   No _____   Unknown _____

Veterinarian's Name _____ Clinical Diagnosis _____

Animal History/Behavior: _____

_____

How did animal die? Killed _____   Natural Causes _____   Other _____   Date of Death _____

Additional information may be written on back.

LABORATORY USE ONLY
1. SPECIMEN: Carcass_____ Head _____ Brain _____ Other _____
METHOD OF SUBMISSION_____
CONDITION OF SPECIMEN _____
2. FLUORESCENT ANTIBODY TEST RESULTS FOR RABIES:
_____ POSITIVE ......Evidence of rabies virus   _____ NEGATIVE....but brain in poor condition. This result does not exclude the possibility of rabies in this animal.
_____NEGATIVE.....No evidence of rabies virus   _____UNSATISFACTORY FOR EXAMINATION
_____ OTHER _____
DATE REPORTED: _____ REPORTED BY: _____
CONTACT_____ CONTACT_____

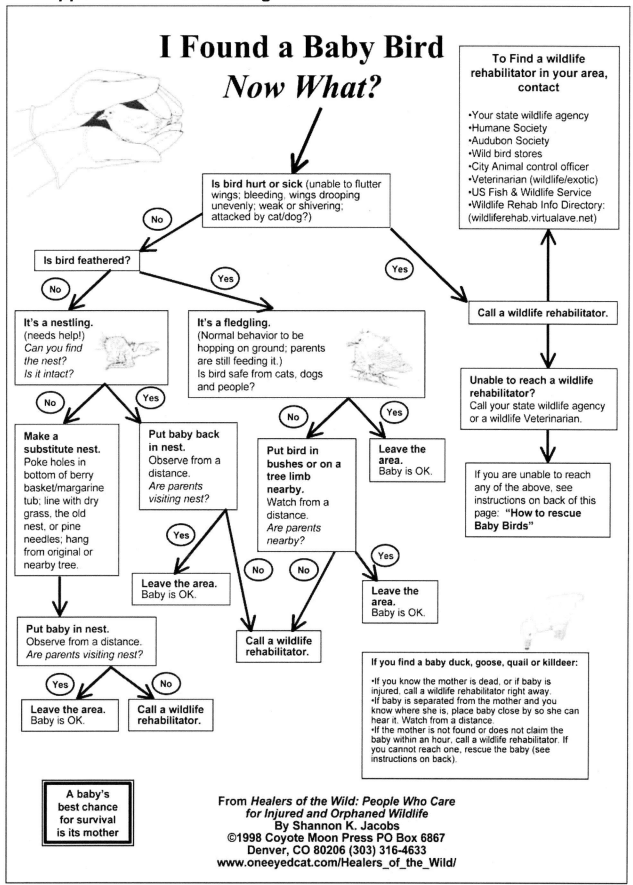

I Found a Baby Bird
Now What?

Is bird hurt or sick (unable to flutter wings; bleeding, wings drooping unevenly; weak or shivering; attacked by cat/dog?)

No → **Is bird feathered?**

Yes → **Call a wildlife rehabilitator.**

To Find a wildlife rehabilitator in your area, contact

- Your state wildlife agency
- Humane Society
- Audubon Society
- Wild bird stores
- City Animal control officer
- Veterinarian (wildlife/exotic)
- US Fish & Wildlife Service
- Wildlife Rehab Info Directory: (wildliferehab.virtualave.net)

No → **It's a nestling.** (needs help!) *Can you find the nest? Is it intact?*

Yes → **It's a fledgling.** (Normal behavior to be hopping on ground; parents are still feeding it.) Is bird safe from cats, dogs and people?

Unable to reach a wildlife rehabilitator? Call your state wildlife agency or a wildlife Veterinarian.

If you are unable to reach any of the above, see instructions on back of this page: **"How to rescue Baby Birds"**

No → **Make a substitute nest.** Poke holes in bottom of berry basket/margarine tub; line with dry grass, the old nest, or pine needles; hang from original or nearby tree.

Yes → **Put baby back in nest.** Observe from a distance. *Are parents visiting nest?*

No → **Put bird in bushes or on a tree limb nearby.** Watch from a distance. *Are parents nearby?*

Yes → **Leave the area.** Baby is OK.

Yes → **Leave the area.** Baby is OK.

Put baby in nest. Observe from a distance. *Are parents visiting nest?*

Call a wildlife rehabilitator.

No / No → **Call a wildlife rehabilitator.**

Yes → **Leave the area.** Baby is OK.

Yes → **Leave the area.** Baby is OK.

No → **Call a wildlife rehabilitator.**

If you find a baby duck, goose, quail or killdeer:

- If you know the mother is dead, or if baby is injured, call a wildlife rehabilitator right away.
- If baby is separated from the mother and you know where she is, place baby close by so she can hear it. Watch from a distance.
- If the mother is not found or does not claim the baby within an hour, call a wildlife rehabilitator. If you cannot reach one, rescue the baby (see instructions on back).

A baby's best chance for survival is its mother

From *Healers of the Wild: People Who Care for Injured and Orphaned Wildlife*
By Shannon K. Jacobs
©1998 Coyote Moon Press PO Box 6867
Denver, CO 80206 (303) 316-4633
www.oneeyedcat.com/Healers_of_the_Wild/

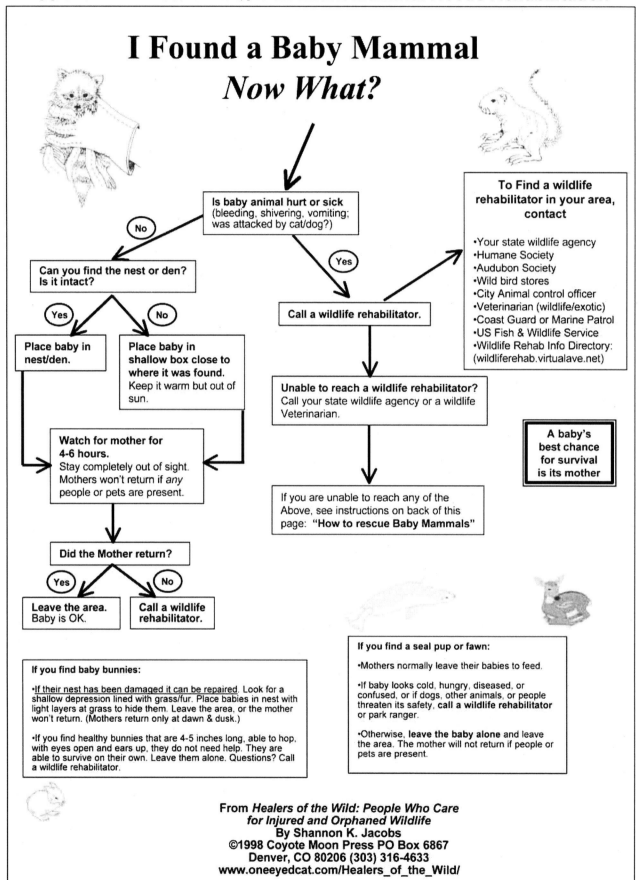

I Found a Baby Mammal
Now What?

Is baby animal hurt or sick (bleeding, shivering, vomiting; was attacked by cat/dog?)

No

Can you find the nest or den? Is it intact?

Yes

No

Place baby in nest/den.

Place baby in shallow box close to where it was found. Keep it warm but out of sun.

Watch for mother for 4-6 hours.
Stay completely out of sight. Mothers won't return if *any* people or pets are present.

Did the Mother return?

Yes

No

Leave the area. Baby is OK.

Call a wildlife rehabilitator.

Yes

Call a wildlife rehabilitator.

Unable to reach a wildlife rehabilitator? Call your state wildlife agency or a wildlife Veterinarian.

If you are unable to reach any of the Above, see instructions on back of this page: "How to rescue Baby Mammals"

To Find a wildlife rehabilitator in your area, contact

• Your state wildlife agency
• Humane Society
• Audubon Society
• Wild bird stores
• City Animal control officer
• Veterinarian (wildlife/exotic)
• Coast Guard or Marine Patrol
• US Fish & Wildlife Service
• Wildlife Rehab Info Directory: (wildliferehab.virtualave.net)

A baby's best chance for survival is its mother

If you find baby bunnies:

•If their nest has been damaged it can be repaired. Look for a shallow depression lined with grass/fur. Place babies in nest with light layers at grass to hide them. Leave the area, or the mother won't return. (Mothers return only at dawn & dusk.)

•If you find healthy bunnies that are 4-5 inches long, able to hop, with eyes open and ears up, they do not need help. They are able to survive on their own. Leave them alone. Questions? Call a wildlife rehabilitator.

If you find a seal pup or fawn:

•Mothers normally leave their babies to feed.

•If baby looks cold, hungry, diseased, or confused, or if dogs, other animals, or people threaten its safety, **call a wildlife rehabilitator** or park ranger.

•Otherwise, **leave the baby alone** and leave the area. The mother will not return if people or pets are present.

From *Healers of the Wild: People Who Care for Injured and Orphaned Wildlife*
By Shannon K. Jacobs
©1998 Coyote Moon Press PO Box 6867
Denver, CO 80206 (303) 316-4633
www.oneeyedcat.com/Healers_of_the_Wild/

Appendix C – References

Introduction & Chapter 1: Current Minimum Standards
Miller, E. A. (ed.) 2006. *NWRA Quick Reference, 3rd edition*. National Wildlife Rehabilitators Association: St. Cloud, MN.

United States Fish & Wildlife Service. Standard Conditions, Special Purpose-Rehabilitation, 50 CFR 21.27. Available from: < http://www.fws.gov/migratorybirds/mbpermits/regulations/regulations.html >.

Chapter 2: Disease Control
Davis, L. 1998. Do You Know How to Disinfect? *The NWRA Quarterly Journal*. 16(3): 10-12.

Clipsham, R. 1990. Environmental Preventive Medicine: Food and Water Management for Reinfection Control. Pp. 87-105 in *Proceedings of the Association of Avian Veterinarians. AAV: Lake Worth, FL*.

Fair, J. M., E. Paul, and J. Jones (eds). 2010. *Guidelines to the Use of Wild Birds in Research, 3rd edition*. The Ornithological Council: Washington, D.C. Available from: < http://www.nmnh.si.edu/BIRDNET/guide/index.html >.

Haufler, J. 1985. Habitat Selection of Release Sites of Rehabilitated or Orphaned Wildlife. *Wildlife Rehabilitation*. 3: 139-143.

Lemarje, R. J., and G. Hosgood. 1995. Antiseptics and Disinfectants in Small Animal Practice. *Compendium on Continuing Education*. 17(11): 1339-1351.

Stokhaug, C. 1988. Selecting Release Sites for Raccoons (*Procyon lotor*). *Wildlife Rehabilitation*. 7: 151-156.

United States Fish & Wildlife Service. Standard Conditions, Special Purpose-Rehabilitation, 50 CFR 21.27. Available from: < http://www.fws.gov/migratorybirds/mbpermits/regulations/regulations.html >.

Chapter 3: General Housing Requirements for Wildlife
Heyn, S. 2000. Behavioral Enrichment for Mammals. *Wildlife Rehabilitation*. 17: 105-112.

Chapter 4: Avian Caging Requirements
Arent, L. R. 2007. *Raptors in Captivity: Guidelines for Care and Management*. Hancock House Publishers: Blaine, WA.

Arent, L. 2000. *Reconditioning Raptors: A Training Manual for the Creance Technique*. The Raptor Center, University of Minnesota: St. Paul, MN.

Arent, L., and M. Martell. 1996. *Care and Management of Captive Raptors*. The Raptor Center, University of Minnesota: St. Paul, MN.

Buhl, G., and L. Borgia (eds.). 2004. *Wildlife in Education: A Guide for the Care and Use of Program Animals*. National Wildlife Rehabilitators Association: St. Cloud, MN.

Chaplin, S. B. 1990. Guidelines for Exercise in Rehabilitated Raptors. *Wildlife Journal.* *12(2):* 17-20.

Forness, M. 1997. Flight Therapy. *The NWRA Quarterly Journal.* 15(3): 7-8.

Gage, L., and R. Duerr (eds.). 2007. *Hand-Rearing Birds.* Blackwell Publishing: Ames, IA.

Gibson, M. J. 1996. The ABC's of Housing Raptors. *Journal of Wildlife Rehabilitation.* *19(3):* 23-31.

Gibson, M. J. 1999. Yours to Protect. *Journal of Wildlife Rehabilitation.* 22(1): 18-26.

Heinemann, J. 1995. Housing Guidelines for Songbirds. *Wildlife Rehabilitation.* 13: 45-66.

Holcomb, J. B. 1988. Net Bottom Caging. *Journal of Wildlife Rehabilitation.* 11(1): 3-4.

Kyle, P., and G. Kyle, 1995. Hand Rearing Chimney Swifts (*Chaetura pelagica*): A 12-Year Retrospective. *Wildlife Rehabilitation.* 13: 95-121.

McKeever, K. 1987. *Care and Rehabilitation of Injured Owls, 4th edition.* The Owl Rehabilitation Research Foundation. W. F. Rannie: Lincoln, ON, Canada.

Sherrod, S. K., W. R. Heinrich, W. A. Burnham, J. H. Barclay, and T. J. Cade. 1982. *Hacking: A Method for Releasing Peregrine Falcons and Other Birds of Prey.* The Peregrine Fund: Boise, ID.

Tegtmeier, S. 2005. General Loon (*Gavia* ssp.) Rehabilitation. *Wildlife Rehabilitation.* 23: 34-48.

Chapter 5: Mammal Caging Requirements

Barnard, S. 1995. *Bats in Captivity.* Available from: < http://www.basicallybats.org/online-book/CONTENTS.htm >.

Burt, W. H., and R. P. Grossenheider. 1976. *A Field Guide to the Mammals of America North of Mexico, 3rd edition.* Houghton Mifflin Co: Boston, MA.

Forness, M. 1984. Raising White-tailed Fawns "Wild." *Journal of Wildlife Rehabilitation.* 7(4): 5-6.

Gage, L., and J. E. Whaley (eds.). 2006. Interim Policies and Best Practices Marine Mammal Stranding Response, Rehabilitation, and Release Standards for Rehabilitation Facilities. NOAA National Marine Fisheries Service: Silver Spring, MD. Available from: < http://www.nmfs.noaa.gov/pr/pdfs/health/rehab_facilities.pdf >

Lecky, J. H. (ed.). 2009. Programmatic Environmental Impact Statement for the Marine Mammal Health and Stranding Response Program. National Marine Fisheries Service: Silver Spring, MD. Available from: < http://www.nmfs.noaa.gov/pr/pdfs/health/eis.pdf >

Lollar, A., and B. Schmidt-French. 1998. *Captive Care and Medical Reference for Rehabilitation of Insectivorous Bats.* Bat World: Mineral Wells, TX.

USDA-APHIS. 9 CFR Ch. 1, Part 3, Subpart E, "Specifications for the Humane Handling, Care, Treatment, and Transportation of Marine Mammals." Office of the Federal Register: Washington, D.C. Available from e-CFR (30 Dec 2009) at < http://ecfr.gpoaccess.gov/cgi/t/ text/text-idx?c=ecfr;sid=02e881d0598f5c6cad31a7b72d9b26e7;rgn=div5;view=text;node=9 %3A1.0.1.1.3;idno=9;cc=ecfr >.

Chapter 6: Reptile Caging Requirements
Association of Zoos &Aquariums. 2008. *Education Standards and Policies.* Association of Zoos & Aquariums: Silver Springs, MD. Available from:
< http://www.aza.org/education-standards-and-policies >.

Bennett, A. F. 1980. The Thermal Dependence of Lizard Behaviour. *Animal Behaviour.* 28(4): 752-762.

Denardo, D. 2006. Stress in Captive Reptiles. Pp. 119-123 in *Reptile Medicine and Surgery* (D. Mader, ed.). W.B. Saunders Company: Philadelphia, PA.

Ernst, C.H., and E.M. Ernst. 2003. *Snakes of the United States and Canada.* Smithsonian Books: Washington, D.C.

Ernst, C.H., and J.E. Lovich. 2009. *Turtles of the United States and Canada.* Johns Hopkins University Press: Baltimore, MD.

Frederick, C. 2000. *Reptile Enrichment Guidelines.* American Association of Zoo Keepers. Available from:
< http://www.aazk.org/committees/enrichment/comm_enrichment_guidelines.php >.

Highfield, A. C. 2002. *Tortoise Trust Foundation Course in Tortoise and Turtle Care.* Online course < www.ttinstitute.co.uk >. Chelonian Educational Resources: London, UK.

Pough, F.H. 1992. *Recommendations for the Care of Amphibians and Reptiles in Academic Institutions.* National Academy Press: Washington, D.C.

Rollin, B.E., and M.L. Kese. 1995. *The Experimental Animal in Biomedical Research. Care, Husbandry, and Well-Being – An Overview by Species.* CRC Press: Boca Raton,FL.

Shepherdson, D.J., J.D. Mellen, and M. Hutchins. (1998). *Second Nature: Environmental Enrichment for Captive Animals.* Smithsonian Institution: Washington, D.C.

Snyder, R.L. 1975. Behavioral Stress in Captive Animals. *Research in Zoos and Aquariums.* National Academy of Sciences: Washington, D.C.

Warwick, C., F. L. Frye, and J.B.Murphy. 1995. *Health and Welfare of Captive Reptiles.* Chapman and Hall: London, UK.

Chapter 7: Final Disposition
Andrews, E. J., B. T. Bennet, J. D. Clark, et al. 1993. Report of the AVMA Panel on Euthanasia. *Journal of the American Veterinary Association.* 202(2): 202-230.

AVMA Guidelines on Euthanasia. 2011. American Veterinary Medical Association. Available at < http://www.avma.org/issues/animal_welfare/euthanasia.pdf >.

Baer, C. K. (ed.) 2006. *Guidelines for Euthanasia of Nondomestic Animals*. American Association of Zoo Veterinarians: Yulee, FL. 111 p. ISBN: 0-689-70726-6. NAL Call Number: SF756.394 .G84 2006. Available from: < http://www.aazv.org/displaycommon. cfm?an=1&subarticlenbr=441 >.

Beaver, B. V., W. Reed, S. Leary, et al. 2000.Report of the AVMA Panel on Euthanasia. *Journal of the American Veterinary Association*. 218(5): 669-696.

Buhl, G., and L. Borgia (eds.). 2004. *Wildlife in Education: A Guide for the Care and Use of Program Animals*. National Wildlife Rehabilitators Association: St. Cloud, MN.

Appendix D – Suggested Reading

Avian Caging
Arent, L. 2000. *Reconditioning Raptors: A Training Manual for the Creance Technique.* The Raptor Center, University of Minnesota: St. Paul, MN.

Arent, L., and M. Martell. 1996. *Care and Management of Captive Raptors.* The Raptor Center, University of Minnesota: St. Paul, MN.

Chaplin, S. B. 1990. Guidelines for Exercise in Rehabilitated Raptors. *Wildlife Journal.* 12(2): 17-20.

Gibson, M. J. 1996. The ABC's of Housing Raptors. *Journal of Wildlife Rehabilitation.* 19(3): 23-31.

Gibson, M. J. 1999. Yours to Protect. *Journal of Wildlife Rehabilitation.* 22(1): 18-26.

Heinemann, J. 1995. Housing Guidelines for Songbirds. *Wildlife Rehabilitation.* 13: 45-66.

Kyle, P., and G. Kyle, 1995. Hand Rearing Chimney Swifts (*Chaetura pelagica*): A 12-Year Retrospective. *Wildlife Rehabilitation.* 13: 95-121.

McKeever, K. 1987. *Care and Rehabilitation of Injured Owls, 4th edition.* The Owl Rehabilitation Research Foundation. W. F. Rannie: Lincoln, ON, Canada.

Orendorff, B. 1997. Hand-rearing Songbirds. *Wildlife Rehabilitation.* 15: 3-40.

Pittel, H. 1994. Care of Adult Songbirds. *Wildlife Rehabilitation.* 12: 83-94.

Iowa Association of Naturalists and Iowa DNR. 1994. Professional Standards for the Use of Live Animals in Environmental Education. Available from: < http://www.ianpage.20m.com/liveanimals.html >.

Redig, P. T. 1993. Methods of Evaluating the Readiness of Rehabilitated Raptors for Release. *Medical Management of Birds of Prey, 2nd edition. The Raptor Center,* University of Minnesota: St. Paul, MN.

Rule, M. 1996. Nutritional Considerations for Captive Songbirds. *Wildlife Rehabilitation.* 14: 75-94.

Smissko, G. 1996. Portable and Permanent Passerine Housing. *Pp. 27-31 in Proceedings of the 1996 IWRC Conference.* International Wildlife Rehabilitation Council: Suisun City, CA.

Definitions/Terminology
Miller, E. A. (ed.) 2006. *NWRA Quick Reference, 3rd edition.* National Wildlife Rehabilitators Association: St. Cloud, MN

Patton, S. 1998. *Wild Words: A Glossary for the Wildlife Rehabilitator, 2nd edition. Wildlife Publications: Maple Valley, WA.*

Disease Control

Calman, R. M., and J. Murray. 1965. *Antibacterial Properties of Chlorhexadine*. Imperial Chemical Industries: London, UK.

Carter, G. R. 1982. *Essentials of Veterinary Bacteriology and Mycology*. Michigan State University Press: East Lansing, MI.

Clipsham, R. 1990. Environmental Preventive Medicine: Food and Water Management for Reinfection Control. Pp. 87-105 in *Proceedings of the Association of Avian Veterinarians. AAV: Lake Worth, FL.*

Davis, L. 1998. Do You Know How to Disinfect? *The NWRA Quarterly Journal.* 16(3): 10-12.

Fair, J. M., E. Paul, and J. Jones (eds). 2010. *Guidelines to the Use of Wild Birds in Research. The Ornithological Council:* Washington, D.C. Available from: < http://www. nmnh.si.edu/BIRDNET/guide/index.html >.

Lawrence, C. A. 1960. Antimicrobial Activity, *in vitro*, of Chlorhexadine, *Journal of the American Pharmaceutical Association.* 49(11): 731-734.

Lemarje, R. J., and G. Hosgood. 1995. Antiseptics and Disinfectants in Small Animal Practice. *Compendium on Continuing Education.* 17(11): 1339-1351.

Over 8,000 Material Safety Data Sheets (MSDS), explaining product toxicity, antidotes, and disposal are available at < http://siri.org/msds/ >.

Final Disposition

Andrews, E. J., B. T. Bennett, et al. Report of the AVMA Panel on Euthanasia. *1993. Journal of the American Veterinary Association.* 202(2): 229-249.

Baer, C. K. (ed.) 2006. *Guidelines for Euthanasia of Nondomestic Animals.* American Association of Zoo Veterinarians: Yulee, FL. 111 p. ISBN: 0-689-70726-6. NAL Call Number: SF756.394 .G84 2006. Available from: < http://www.aazv.org/displaycommon. cfm?an=1&subarticlenbr=441 >.

Martell, M. 1994. Analyzing Habitat for Release of Rehabilitated Animals. *Wildlife Rehabilitation.* 12: 191-197.

General Housing Requirements for Wildlife

Institute of Laboratory Animal Resources. 1991. *Education and Training in the Care and Use of Laboratory Animals: A Guide for Developing Institutional Programs.* National Academy of Sciences, Committee on Educational Programs in Laboratory Animal Science, Washington, DC: National Academy Press, 139 pp. NAL call number: SF604.E3.

Institute of Laboratory Animal Resources, Commission on Life Sciences, National Research Council. 1996. *Guide for the Care and Use of Laboratory Animals, 7th Ed.* Washington, D.C.: National Academy Press, 125p. NAL call number: SF406.G95 1996. Available from: < http://www.nap.edu/openbook.php?record_id=5140 >.

Heyn, S. 2000. Behavioral Enrichment for Mammals. *Wildlife Rehabilitation.* 17: 105-112.

Mammal Caging

Barnard, S. 1995. *Bats in Captivity*. Available from: < http://www.basicallybats.org/online-book/CONTENTS.htm >.

USDA-APHIS. 9 CFR Ch. 1, Part 3, Subpart E, "Specifications for the Humane Handling, Care, Treatment, and Transportation of Marine Mammals." Office of the Federal Register: Washington, D.C. Available from e-CFR (30 Dec 2009) at
< http://ecfr.gpoaccess.gov/cgi/t/text/text-idx?c=ecfr;sid=02e881d0598f5c6cad31a7b72d9b26e7;rgn=div5;view=text;node=9%3A1.0.1.1.3;idno=9;cc=ecfr >.

Forness, M. 1984. Raising White-tailed Fawns "Wild." *Journal of Wildlife Rehabilitation.* 7(4):5-6.

Lollar, A., and B. Schmidt-French. 1998. *Captive Care and Medical Reference for Rehabilitation of Insectivorous Bats*. Bat World: Mineral Wells, TX.

Taylor, P. 1995. *Opossum Orphan Care Training Manual*. Opossum Society of the United States: Huntington Beach, CA.

Whaley, J. E. 2009. National Template: Marine Mammal Stranding Agreement Between National Marine Fisheries Service Of The National Oceanic and Atmospheric Administration Department Of Commerce and [Stranding Network Organization]. National Marine Fisheries Service: Silver Spring, MD. Available from: < http://www.nmfs.noaa.gov/pr/pdfs/health/eis_appendixc.pdf >.

Reptiles

Blankenship, A. 2005. Reptile Cage Cleaning 101. Cross Timbers Herpetologist newsletter. Available from: < http://www.zooniversity.org/pdf/XTimbersHerpNov05CageClean.pdf >.

Funk, R. 2006. Snakes. Pp. 42-58 in *Reptile Medicine and Surgery* (D. Mader, ed.). W.B. Saunders Company: Philadelphia, PA.

Mader, D. (ed.) 2006. *Reptile Medicine and Surgery.* W.B. Saunders Company: Philadelphia, PA.

Wissman, M.A. 2007. *Cleaning Reptile Cages*. Available from:
< http://www.reptilechannel.com/reptile-health/cleaning-snake-cages.aspx >.

American Association of Zoo Keepers Enrichment Committee at
< www.aazk.org/committees/enrichment/comm_enrichment_title.php >.

The Shape of Enrichment at < www.enrichment.org >.

The Tortoise Trust at < www.tortoisetrust.org >. (Numerous articles on housing for turtles and tortoises).

Appendix E – Manufacturers of Products Mentioned

Astroturf®	American Sports Products Group, Inc., White Plains, NY
Avinol-3™	Veterinary Products Laboratory, Phoenix, AZ
Bed-a-beast™	Pet-Tech Products, Van Nuys, CA
Betadine® Solution & Scrub	Purdue Fredrick Company, Norwalk, CT
Bio-Rite®	Damon Industries, Inc., Alliance, OH
Calci-sand™	T-Rex®, Chula Vista, CA
Carefresh®	Absorption Corp, Ferndale, WA
Caterpillar Castle®	Live Monarch Foundation, Boca Raton, FL
ChlorhexiDerm Disinfectant®	DVM Pharmaceuticals, Inc, Miami, FL
Cidex®	Johnson & Johnson Medical, Ethicon, Inc., Arlington, TX
Cleansing Gele'	Oxyfresh Worldwide, Inc., Coeur d'Alene, ID
Clorox®	The Clorox Company, Oakland, CA
Con-Tact® Brand Grip Liner	Kittrich Corp., La Mirada, CA
Dent-a-gene	Oxyfresh Worldwide, Inc., Coeur d'Alene, ID
Dioxi Care®	Frontier Pharmaceuticals, Inc., Melville, NY
Dri-Dek®	Kendall Products, Naples, FL
Hexol®	Hexol Inc., Alpharetta, GA
Kennel Kare™	Health Technology Professional Products, Riverside, CA
Kennelsol®	Alpha Tech Pet, Inc., Lexington, MA
Lysol®	Reckitt Benckiser, Berks, England
Nolvasan®	Wyeth Pharmaceuticals, Collegeville, PA
Nomad™	3M Company, St. Paul, MN
1-Stroke Environ®	Steris Corporation, Mentor, OH
Oxine® (AH)	Bio-Cide International, Norman, OK
Parvosol®	Hess & Clark, Inc., Randolph, WI
Pine-Sol®	The Clorox Company, Oakland, CA
Port-A-Bat®	Dynamic Creations of USA, Goodyear, AZ
Purex®	Henkel Corporation, Scottsdale, AZ

Minimum Standards for Wildlife Rehabilitation, 4th edition, 2012, NWRA & IWRC

Quinticare™	(formerly Quinticide™) Schroer Manufacturing Co., Kansas City, MO
Reptarium®	Dallas Manufacturing Co., Dallas, TX
Roccal®-D	The Upjohn Company, Kalamazoo, MI
Virosan® Bio-Ceutic	Boehringer Ingelheim Vetmedica, Inc., St. Joseph, MO
Wavicide®	Medical Chemical Corporation, Torrance, CA

Appendix F – Unit Conversion Table

To change	To	Multiply by
centimeters	inches	.3937
centimeters	feet	.03281
feet	meters	.3048
gallons (US)	liters	3.7853
grams	ounces	.0353
grams	pounds	.002205
inches	millimeters	25.4000
inches	centimeters	2.5400
kilograms	pounds	2.2046
liters	gallons (US)	.2642
liters	pints	2.1134
liters	quarts	1.0567
meters	feet	3.2808
meters	yards	1.0936
milliliters	tablespoons	.0667
millimeters	inches	.0394
ounces	grams	28.3495
ounces	milliliters	30
ounces	pounds	.0625
pints	liters	.4732
pounds	kilograms	.4536
pounds	ounces	16
quarts	liters	.9463
square feet	square meters	.0929
square meters	square feet	10.7639
square meters	square yards	1.1960
square yards	square meters	.8361
tablespoon	milliliters	15
yards	meters	.9144

To change	To	
Celsius	Fahrenheit	multiply by 1.8 and add 32
Fahrenheit	Celsius	subtract 32 and multiply by 0.55

Minimum Standards for Wildlife Rehabilitation, 4th edition, 2012, NWRA & IWRC